Bilingual edition: German and English

Canadian Escapades - Kanadische Eskapaden

The true story
of the author's 3 escapes
from WW2 POW camps

Klaus Conrad

Visit **can-esc.com** for the latest news and links

Published by Germancosm

Translated by Maximilian Franck and Scott S. Lawton

Published by Germancosm; an imprint of PreFab Software, Inc.
24 Colonial Dr, Chelmsford, MA 01824

First Germancosm printing: November 2009

Printed in the United States of America

Translated by Maximilian Franck and Scott S. Lawton

Cover designed by Scott S. Lawton (with lots of feedback from others)
and produced by Kyle Orosz; Copyright 2009 by Germancosm

Publisher's Cataloging-in-Publication Data

Conrad, Klaus, 1917–

Canadian Escapades - Kanadische Eskapaden : the true story of the author's 3 escapes from WW2 POW camps / written by Klaus Conrad ; translated by Maximilian Franck and Scott S. Lawton.

— Bilingual ed., German and English, aligned by sentence.

p.   cm.

ISBN 978-0-9843271-0-2 (pbk.)

1. German language and literature monographs.   2. Prisoner of war escapes —Canada—History—20th Century.   3. Adventures and adventurers.   4. World War, 1939-1945—Personal narratives—German.   I. Title

D805.C2.C6 2009

940.54/72—dc22

2009940552

Image Credits

The following 2 people were kind enough to make their photos available to all under a Creative Commons "by" attribution license (http://creativecommons.org/licenses/by/2.0/deed.en), including taking the risk that adaptations do not do justice to the originals.

- jmegjmeg: "freight car + burner" (http://www.flickr.com/photos/75842363@N00/2508511117/)
- MarmotChaser: "Autumn in Pennsylvania" (http://www.flickr.com/photos/9702212@N03/2946009570/)

Thanks also to Flickr for providing a CC-BY search page.

The pocket watch (http://www.clker.com/clipart-15103.html) and barbed wire snippet (http://www.clker.com/clipart-barbed-wire.html) were posted to Clker by OCAL. The site is a very useful source of public domain clip art.

The map of North America is adapted from the CIA World Factbook. As with most US Government publications, the original is in the public domain.

Introduction

This first edition, quite intentionally, **preserves the author's informal style**, including long sentences with several ideas joined by commas, as may be more appropriate for retelling the story in front of a campfire, but which, like this sentence, surely exceed what might otherwise be expected in print. Some compound sentences have been split to make the dual-language alignment more clear – though the lines that start with a lowercase letter may stand out a bit. If enough readers express a preference for the usual conventions of print, we may release a new edition.

We may also release an English-only edition in the future. Meanwhile, I hope that readers who aren't interested in German will still enjoy what I think is a great story.

For those who are interested in language, I made the translation into English as literal as I could while trying to follow English rules and style. Feedback welcome! (The first two translation passes were done by others, but any awkwardness that remains may well be my doing.)

The format of this **bilingual edition** is designed to encourage those who are still learning the other language (whether English or German) to read the story in that language. If you don't understand a sentence after reading it carefully, just glance at the other column. **No tedious dictionary lookup is required.** (Tip: but otherwise keep that side covered. It's too easy to get wrapped up in the story and continue in whichever language you find easier. To quote from the book: "die schönsten Früchte fallen uns nicht mühelos in den Schoß".)

Scott S. Lawton
November 2009

P.S. I should probably disclose that, although related only by marriage, Dr. Klaus Conrad is my uncle's uncle. I've met him twice, but only recently learned of his adventures -- and, more importantly, that he had written them down several years ago for family and friends. I'm pleased to take the opportunity to present his escapades to a wider audience.

After being shot down over England in 1941, German Air Force officer Klaus Conrad was captured as a prisoner of war. He was taken to Canada in 1942. This story begins in March 1945 at a POW camp near the town of Wainwright, Alberta. Although the first POWs arrived at the camp on January 29, 1945, construction work on the fence continued for several months.

I

Endlich waren alle Vorbereitungen abgeschlossen.

Finally all preparations were completed.

Fieberhaft hatte ein kleiner Kreis Eingeweihter Tag und Nacht mitgeholfen, alle die vielen Dinge, die zu einer Flucht gehörten, fertigzustellen.

Feverishly, a small circle of insiders had helped day and night to complete all the many things needed for an escape.

Aus alten Decken waren Zivilanzüge entstanden, Arbeitermützen waren gefertigt, Karten gezeichnet, Ausweise gefälscht und sogar etwas Geld aufgetrieben worden.

Old blankets were turned into civilian clothing, worker hats were made, maps drawn, IDs forged and even some money was obtained.

Seit Wochen schon hatten wir die Gewohnheiten der einzelnen Wachposten genau studiert und uns ihren Wachturnus gemerkt.

For weeks we had closely studied the habits of every guard and memorized their shifts.

Da gab es Schläfrige und Wachsame, Unpünktliche und Genaue, solche, die sich durch das geringste Geräusch gleich in Aufregung versetzen ließen und sofort schössen, und andere, die im Stehen zu schlafen verstanden.

There were sleepy and alert guards, tardy and punctual guards, some who would get agitated by the slightest noise and immediately shoot, and others who tried to sleep standing up.

Die letzte Morgenzählung

Etwas beklommen, nach links und rechts schielend, wohnten wir noch der Morgenzählung bei – zum letzten Male!

Der diensthabende Sergeant schritt die Reihen entlang – für den Bruchteil einer Sekunde ruhten seine Augen in den meinen; ahnte er etwas?

Mir war plötzlich ganz trocken in der Kehle

– schon war er vorbei; die nächste Kolonne, die übernächste.

„Zählung beendet!" ertönte der Ruf.

„Nun aber schnell!" sagte Heinz, „wenn's jetzt klappt, dann sucht uns niemand mehr bis zur Abendzählung um 5 Uhr – und dann sind wir über alle Berge …"

Rasch hatten wir unsere Zivilanzüge angezogen und darüber blaue Overalls gestreift, wie sie von jedem Arbeiter in Nordamerika getragen werden.

Schlecht rasiert und ein wenig geschminkt, um älter auszusehen, schlenderten wir über den Lagersportplatz, steckten eine Tragstange durch eine Stacheldrahtrolle, die von Zaunausbesserungen liegengeblieben war und schritten damit zum Tor.

The last morning count

Quite anxious, glancing right and left, we attended the morning count – for the last time!

The sergeant on duty was walking along the rows – for a split-second his eyes met mine; did he suspect something?

It was suddenly quite dry in my throat

– then he passed by; to the next column, then the one after that.

"Count finished!" the call sounded.

"Now; quickly!" said Heinz, "if it works now, then nobody will look for us until the evening count at 5 o'clock – and then we'll be far away …"

Quickly we had put on our civilian clothes and then blue striped overalls, the kind worn by every worker in North America.

Badly shaven and with a little makeup to look older, we sauntered across the camp's sports field, stuck a bar through a roll of barbed wire that was left behind after fence repair work, and strode with it to the gate.

Als wir auf Rufweite heranwaren, wurde gerade ein Arbeiter von außen hereingelassen; er glaubte, zwei seiner Arbeitskollegen kommen zu sehen, und machte Anstalten, auf uns zu warten.

Once we were within earshot, a worker was being let in from outside; he thought he saw two of his coworkers coming, and proceeded to wait for us.

„Der hat uns gerade noch gefehlt!" flüsterte Heinz hinter mir.

"That's the last thing we needed!" whispered Heinz behind me.

Wir legten die Drahtrolle ab und machten uns an ihr zu schaffen, bis dem Wartenden die Zeit zu lang wurde und er von dannen trottete.

We set the wire roll down and started fiddling around with it, until the time dragged on too long for the waiting worker and he trotted away.

Erleichtert setzten wir unseren Weg fort.

Relieved, we continued on our way.

Kaltblütig schritten wir auf den diensthabenden Posten zu, als seien wir schon hundertmal diesen Weg gegangen.

Coolly we strode toward the guard on duty, as if we had gone this way a hundred times before.

Wie würde er sich verhalten?

How would he react?

Interessiert schaute er uns entgegen.

Interested, he looked over at us.

Wenn er nur kein Gespräch mit uns anfängt!

If only he wouldn't start a conversation with us!

Wir waren aufs höchste gespannt; nur wenige Schritte trennten uns – da näherte sich von außen her ein Offizier.

We had the utmost anxiety; very few steps remained – then an officer approached from outside.

Dienstbeflissen eilte der Soldat ans äußere Tor.

Diligent in his duty, the soldier hurried toward the outer gate.

Während er es umständlich aufschloß, traten wir durch das offene Tor des inneren Zaunringes und gelangten unbehelligt in den schmalen Gang zwischen den beiden Zäunen.

While he laboriously opened it, we stepped through the open gate of the inner fence ring and arrived unharmed in the narrow path between the two fences.

Einen Zaun hatten wir überwunden, aber der zweite äußere trennte uns noch von der Freiheit.

We had passed one fence, but the second, outer, still separated us from freedom.

Langsam schritten wir weiter, hier und da stehen bleibend, um die Festigkeit eines Pfostens oder Drahtstranges zu prüfen.

Slowly we strode along, stopping here and there to check the strength of a post or wire.

„Hey, you!" rief ein Posten vom Eckturm uns an; „What are you doing?"

"Hey, you!" a guard called to us from the corner tower; "What are you doing?"

„Der diensthabende Sergeant habe uns zu Ausbesserungsarbeiten am Zaun bestellt", gaben wir in breitem Amerikanisch zur Antwort.

"The sergeant on duty told us to perform repair work on the fence," was the answer we gave – in a broad American accent.

„Aber ihr seid nicht gemeldet!"

"But you're not registered!"

„Must be a mistake; wir werden auf der Wache Bescheid sagen."

"Must be a mistake; we'll inform the guardhouse."

Ruhig setzten wir uns wieder zur Wache hin in Bewegung.

Calmly, we started moving back toward the guardhouse again.

Plötzlich blieben wir stehen – etwas zu rasch vielleicht.

Suddenly we stopped – perhaps somewhat too quickly.

Der diensthabende Sergeant selber kam auf uns zu; vor ihm konnte unsere Ausrede nichts helfen.

The sergeant on duty himself came toward us; with him our excuse wouldn't help at all.

Er kannte Heinz, den Lagerdolmetscher, er kannte mich von zwei früheren Fluchtversuchen her.

He knew Heinz, the camp's interpreter, he knew me from two earlier escape attempts.

Wir wandten die Gesichter ab.

We turned our faces away.

Aus dem Lager ertönte ein Pfiff – das verabredete Zeichen, daß alles verloren sei und Karten, Ausweise und Geld zu vernichten seien, um sie nicht bei der Festnahme in die Hände der Kanadier fallen zu lassen.

A whistle sounded from the camp – the agreed-upon signal that everything was lost and that maps, IDs and money were to be destroyed, so they wouldn't fall into the hands of the Canadians if we were caught.

Nervös zündeten wir uns eine Zigarette an, ein kleines Päckchen fiel zur Erde, wurde mit dem Fuß verscharrt.

Nervously we each lit a cigarette, let a small package fall to the ground to bury with our feet.

Der Schweiß brach uns aus allen Poren – so schnell sollte unsere Flucht enden?

Sweat broke out from every pore – should our escape end so quickly?

Nach einer halben Stunde bereits?

After only half an hour?

– und vier Wochen Arrest waren uns sicher.

– and four weeks of confinement were certain.

Warum kam der Sergeant nicht?

Why was the sergeant not coming?

Ließ er sicherheitshalber noch den Korporal kommen?

Was he calling for the corporal to be on the safe side?

Kaum wagten wir uns wieder umzudrehen; als wir es taten, da war der Sergeant in einer der nächsten Baracken verschwunden.

We hardly dared to turn around again; once we did, the sergeant had disappeared into one of the nearby barracks.

„Heißer Boden!" sagte Heinz.

"What a hot spot!" said Heinz.

Er zog einen Hammer aus der Tasche und klopfte geschäftig an einem der Zaunpfähle.

He pulled a hammer out of the bag and hammered busily on one of the fence posts.

Ich bückte mich, hob das inhaltsschwere Päckchen wieder auf.

I bent over, picked up the small package that contained such momentous contents.

Der Posten auf dem Turm wurde unruhig.

The guard on the tower was getting agitated.

Ja, richtig, wir hatten auf der Wache Bescheid über unser Tun zu geben.

Yes, right, we were to inform the guardhouse of our task.

Alles hat nach Vorschrift zu gehen, darin sind sich alle Armeen der Welt gleich.

Everything had to go by the book, in that, all armies of the world are the same.

Also zurück zum Tor und zur Wache.

So, back to the gate and to the guardhouse.

Betont lässig, die Zigarette im Mundwinkel, jeden Gleichschritt vermeidend, machten wir uns auf den Weg.

Deliberately nonchalant, cigarettes in the corners of our mouths, avoiding a lockstep march, we started on our way.

Plötzlich Musik aus dem Lager …

Suddenly, music from the camp …

Die Lagerkapelle spielte den neuesten amerikanischen Schlager.

The camp band was playing the latest American hits.

„Crazy P/W's" – „verrückte Kriegsgefangene", hörten wir einen Posten sagen, als wir an der Wache vorbeikamen.

"Crazy P/Ws," we heard a guard say as we passed by the guardhouse.

Aber der Zweck war erreicht – die Wache war abgelenkt worden, nahm keine weitere Notiz von uns.

But the purpose was accomplished – the guardhouse was distracted, took no further notice of us.

„Hoffentlich haben wir auf dieser Seite mehr Glück!" murmelte ich, als wir die Wache hinter uns hatten – und jetzt schien es tatsächlich zu klappen.

"Hopefully we'll have more luck on this side!" I muttered as we left the guardhouse behind us – and now it actually seemed to work.

Geschäftig klopfte Heinz wieder an den Zaunpfählen, während ich mit einem Spreizholz zwei Drähte auseinandersperrte.

Heinz busily hammered on the fence posts again, while I separated two wires with a spreader board.

Dann – das Herz schlug mir bis zum Hals – schlüpfte ich hindurch, während der Posten vom Wachturm gemächlich zuschaute, ließ mir den Hammer reichen und schlug auf der anderen Seite einen Nagel ins Holz.

Then – my heart pounding in my throat – I slid through while the guard from the watchtower leisurely watched, reached for the hammer and pounded a nail into the wood on the other side.

Darauf schoben wir unsere Drahtrolle durch den Zaun.

Then we pushed our roll of wire through the fence.

Heinz folgte.

Heinz followed.

Auf der Außenseite spannten wir ein paar Drähte und nagelten sie fest.

On the outer side we ran a few wires and nailed them firmly.

Dann – alles Werkzeug liegen lassend, als ob wir gleich wiederkommen würden – entfernten wir uns …

Then – leaving all the tools behind as if we were to return soon – we departed …

Krachte da ein Schuß?

Was a shot fired?

Nein, es war nur ein Hund, der bellte …

No, it was just a dog, that barked …

Mit Mühe gelang es uns, unsere gemächliche Gangart beizubehalten – bis zum Zerreißen angespannt waren die Nerven – würde es klappen …?

With effort we managed to maintain our leisurely pace – our nerves were stretched to the breaking point – would it work …?

Noch wenige Meter, dann waren wir in Deckung des nächsten Gebüschs.

Only a few meters, then we were under the cover of the next bushes.

Bald hatten wir die Bahnlinie überschritten und die Hauptstraße nach Edmonton erreicht.

Soon we had crossed the railroad tracks and reached the main road into Edmonton.

Wir waren frei.

We were free.

7

II

Per Anhalter nach Edmonton

Eine unbeschreibliche Freude überkam uns, während wir mit jeder Minute unseren Abstand zum Lager vergrößerten.

In diesen Augenblicken kam uns der Begriff „Freiheit" so recht zum Bewußtsein.

Das Glücksgefühl über den gelungenen Ausbruch beflügelte unsere Schritte, und wir begannen vor Freude zu laufen.

„Was werden die für Augen machen, wenn sie merken, daß zwei fehlen", frohlockte Heinz, als wir endlich verschnauften.

Hitchhiking to Edmonton

An indescribable feeling of joy overcame us, as, with every passing minute, we increased our distance from the camp.

In these moments, the concept "freedom" came so directly into our consciousness.

The feeling of happiness from the successful escape quickened our steps, and we began running out of joy.

"How surprised they're going to be when they notice that two are missing," rejoiced Heinz, when we finally paused for breath.

„Den Sergeanten möchte ich sehen, wenn er feststellt, daß ich ihm schon wieder durchgegangen bin", entgegnete ich „aber ein verdammtes Gefühl in der Kehle war das, als er vorhin auf uns zukam.

Und noch sind wir in bedrohlicher Nähe des Lagers, hoffentlich kommt bald ein Auto und nimmt uns mit."

„Per Anhalter fahren" ist ein etwas umständlicher deutscher Ausdruck.

Er ist sicherlich noch nicht alt.

Die Amerikaner haben ein Verbum dafür: „to hitchhike", und das zeigt, wie gang und gäbe bei ihnen diese Reisemethode ist.

Wir gingen also die Straße entlang und bald kam auch ein etwas klappriger Wagen, der sofort bereitwillig anhielt.

„Going to Edmonton?" – „Fahren Sie nach Edmonton?"

„That's right", sagte der einzige Insasse und nahm uns mit.

Er war ein junger Mann, kaum älter als wir selber, und übrigens voll strotzender Gesundheit.

Wieso war er nicht Soldat?

"I want to see the sergeant when he finds out that I've slipped through his fingers again," I replied "but I had such a damned feeling in my throat when he was approaching us earlier.

We're still dangerously close to the camp, hopefully a car comes soon and takes us along."

"Per Anhalter fahren" is a somewhat circuitous German expression.

It certainly can't be very old yet.

The Americans have a verb for it: "to hitchhike," and that shows how commonplace this method of travel is with them.

So we went alongside the road and soon a somewhat rickety car came along, that immediately stopped, unhesitant.

"Going to Edmonton?"

"That's right," said the sole occupant and took us with him.

He was a young man, barely older than us and, incidentally, brimming with health.

How was he not a soldier?

Die gleiche Frage mochte er sich in Bezug auf uns beide vorlegen, denn bald begann er eine Unterhaltung und fragte so viel, daß wir achtgeben mußten, uns nicht in Widersprüche zu verwickeln.

He might have been asking himself the same question about us, because soon he started a conversation and asked so much that we must be careful not to get entangled in contradictions.

Es war am späten Nachmittag, als wir in Edmonton, der Hauptstadt Albertas und Metropole Nord-West-Kanadas eintrafen.

It was late afternoon when we reached Edmonton, the capital of Alberta and metropolis of Northwestern Canada.

Teils unserem eigenen Hunger, teils der freundlichen Aufforderung unseres Fahrers folgend, suchten wir eine kleine Speisebar auf.

Partly because of our own hunger, partly because of the driver's friendly invitation, we found a little diner.

Beklommenen Herzens traten wir ein, denn wir hatten ja so gut wie kein Geld außer den paar Silbermünzen, die von illegalen Tauschgeschäften mit kanadischen Posten im Lager stammten.

We entered with anxious hearts, since we had as good as no money except the few silver coins from our illegal trading activities with the Canadian guards inside the camp.

An der Theke bekamen wir Kaffee, Sandwiches und ein paar Eier, und als wir verlegen mit unseren wenigen Münzen klimperten, da bezahlte der junge Mann die Rechnung für uns mit.

At the counter we were served coffee, sandwiches and some eggs, and when we sheepishly jingled our few coins the young man paid the bill for us.

Es schlug sechs.

The clock struck six.

In jähem Schrecken sahen wir uns an.

In sudden fear, we looked at each other.

Vor einer Stunde war Zählung gewesen im Kriegsgefangenenlager Wainwright …

An hour ago the count had taken place in the Wainwright POW camp …

und wenn es mit den beiden Strohpuppen und ihren aufgesetzten Gipsköpfen, die bei der Zählung im dritten Glied mitgeführt wurden, nicht geklappt hatte, dann mußte uns die Polizei schon auf den Fersen sein.

Anfang des Krieges, da hatten wir einmal mit einer solchen Puppe den Ausbruch eines Kameraden fünf Tage lang tarnen können – aber seither hatten auch unsere Bewachungsmannschaften allerlei dazu gelernt.

Während der Zählung mußte jede Kolonne nach dem Abschreiten der Front durch den zählenden Sergeanten mehrere Schritte vorrücken

– und ob die beiden mitgeführten Puppen mit ihren künstlichen Gelenken das mitmachen würden, ohne aufzufallen, war die Frage.

Auf welche Ideen waren wir nicht schon gekommen, um die Kanadier bei den Zählungen zu täuschen;

Köpfe aus Gips, aus Holz und aus Pappmachee waren modelliert worden,

im Krankenrevier lagen lebensgroße Puppen, deren Brust sich in regelmäßigen Abständen hob und senkte, betätigt durch eine feine Schnur, die zum Nachbarbett führte,

and if the two hay dolls with their gypsum heads that replaced us in the third column hadn't done the job, the police must already be on our heels.

At the beginning of the war we were able to cover a comrade's escape with such a dummy for five days – but the guard teams had learned a lot since then.

During the count, every column had to move a few steps forward after the inspection of the front by the counting sergeant

– and whether the two carried dolls with their artificial joints would take part without being noticed – that was the question.

Such ideas had we not already thought up to deceive the Canadians at roll call;

gypsum heads on dummies modeled out of wood and paper mache,

in the sick bay lay life-sized dolls, whose chests moved up and down at regular intervals, operated by a thin cord leading to the neighboring bed,

kunstvolle Falltüren waren in die Fußböden geschnitten worden, um bei Zählungen im Haus unbemerkt von einem Stockwerk ins andere zu gelangen – um sich dort anstelle des fehlenden Kameraden zum zweiten Male zählen zu lassen.

Plötzlich wurden wir in unseren Gedanken unterbrochen; das Radioprogramm, das geräuschvoll aus dem Lautsprecher tönte – brach ab.

Würden wir jetzt unseren Steckbrief hören?

Die Eier schmeckten uns auf einmal nicht mehr.

Auch nicht der Whisky, den unser Freund uns noch hinterher spendierte.

Augenzwinkernd gestand er uns, er sei ein Deserteur.

Aber als wir ihm nicht die Bruderhand reichten, die er wohl erwartet hatte, da wurde ihm, dem legalen Kanadier, anscheinend bange vor seiner Redseligkeit – und er verabschiedete sich rasch.

Daß er auch uns für Deserteure gehalten hatte, war gar nicht so verwunderlich, denn zu jener Zeit hielten sich in den Wäldern Nordkanadas viele Deserteure auf,

vornehmlich Franco-Kanadier aus den französischen Provinzen Kanadas, die sich geweigert hatten, nach Übersee zu gehen.

artful trap doors cut into the floors to be able to move unnoticed from one floor to another while a count was going on in the house – to be counted there a second time in place of the missing comrade.

Suddenly our thoughts were interrupted; the radio program that boomed noisily from the speakers – broke off.

Would we now hear our escape announced?

All of a sudden the eggs no longer tasted good.

Nor did the whiskey that our friend had sprung for afterward.

Winking, he confessed to us: he was a deserter.

But when we didn't accept his brotherly handshake, which he had indeed expected, then he, the legal Canadian, seemed to regret that he was so talkative – and he made a quick farewell.

That he took us for fellow deserters wasn't surprising, because at that time, many deserters were staying in the woods of Northern Canada,

mainly Franco-Canadians from the French provinces of Canada, who had refused to go overseas.

Bald befanden wir uns wieder auf der Landstraße und marschierten rüstig gen Norden.

Soon we found ourselves back on the country road and marching vigorously northward.

Noch einmal wurden wir ein Stück Wegs mitgenommen.

Once again we found a ride for part of the way.

Schnell wurde es Nacht.

Quickly it became night.

Ein Strohschober diente als Lager.

A haystack served as camp.

Wir waren bald eingeschlafen.

We had soon fallen asleep.

Plötzlich fuhren wir hoch.

Suddenly, we shot up.

Ein langgezogenes Heulen hatte uns geweckt.

A long drawn out howl had awakened us.

Jetzt vernahmen wir es wieder – ganz nahe – und dazwischen ein merkwürdiges Kläffen.

We heard it again – very close – and a strange yapping in between.

Präriehunde, eine Schakalart, mußten es sein.

It must be wild dogs, some type of jackal.

„Stehen wir auf", meinte Heinz, „zum Schlafen kommen wir doch nicht mehr bei der Kälte."

"Let's get up," suggested Heinz, "we won't be getting back to sleep in this cold."

Wir fröstelten und rieben die klammen Hände.

We were freezing and rubbed our damp hands.

„Zu dumm, daß wir wegen der enggespannten Drähte nicht mehr anziehen konnten", bemerkte ich „aber das Durchschlüpfen durch den Zaun war schon so schwierig genug gewesen."

"Too bad that because of the narrowly spanned wires we couldn't put on more clothes," I remarked "but slipping through the fence was already hard enough."

Im Dunkeln trotteten wir auf der Landstraße weiter, die wie ausgestorben schien.

In the dark, we jogged farther along the country road, which seemed deserted.

Kein Fahrzeug kam um diese Stunde daher.

No car came along at this hour.

Endlich wurde es Tag.

Finally it became day.

Gleich der erste Lkw, dem wir winkten, nahm uns mit.

The first truck that we waived down gave us a ride.

Immer weiter nach Norden gelangten wir, immer tiefer in die riesigen Waldgebiete Nord-West-Kanadas.

Ever farther to the north we went, ever deeper into the vast forested areas of Northwest Canada.

Wälder, Wälder, soweit das Auge reichte, dazwischen einige Seen, hin und wieder ein Gehöft, ganz selten eine Ortschaft.

Forests, forests, as far as the eye could see, some lakes in between, now and again a farmhouse, quite seldom a town.

Der Urwald begann ...

The wilderness began ...

Am Nachmittag erreichten wir Athabasca.

In the afternoon, we reached Athabasca.

Letzter Ausläufer der Zivilisation, eine Sägemühle, ein Kino, eine Bar – und dann beginnt der Urwald endgültig seine Herrschaft.

The last outpost of civilization, a sawmill, a theater, a bar – and then the wild forest finally began its reign.

Weiter nach Norden führte nur ein ganz selten befahrener Weg.

The only way to go farther north was a rarely used path.

Es war wirklich ein großer Zufall, daß ein Trapper mit seinem Vehikel daherkam und uns mitnahm.

It was really a great coincidence, that a trapper came along with his vehicle and gave us a ride.

Diese Breiten sind so dünn besiedelt, daß jedes fremde Gesicht sofort auffällt.

These zones are so sparsely populated, that every strange face immediately stands out.

Wie ein Inquisitor fragte uns der neuigkeitshungernde Mann aus – und was wußten denn wir von der Welt außerhalb des Stacheldrahtes?

Like an inquisitor, the news-starved man questioned us – but what did we know of the world outside the barbed wire?

15

Zum Glück war der Trapper selbst sehr redselig, denn er hatte scheinbar selten Gelegenheit, sich zu unterhalten.

So erfuhren wir bald alles Wissenswerte über das Land zwischen Athabasca und Peace River, einer Ortschaft einige hundert Meilen weiter nördlich.

„Well, boys, ich glaube, wir werden uns bald wiedersehen", meinte der Trapper, als er uns gegen Abend an einem Seitenweg absetzte und machte ein vielsagendes Gesicht.

„Was er wohl gemeint hat mit diesen Worten beim Abschied", bemerkte ich nach einer Weile, als wir schon ein gutes Stück waldeinwärts marschiert waren.

„Und dieses merkwürdige Mienenspiel um seine Augen, als wenn er ..."

Heinz sprach nicht weiter, und jeder hing seinen Gedanken nach; irgendein unangenehmes Gefühl beschlich mich aber, sooft ich an den Trapper dachte.

Wir kamen gut vorwärts auf unserem Weg, denn ein Schneepflug hatte den Schnee geräumt; als es zu dämmern begann, waren wir nur noch etwa zwei Stunden von dem Holzfällerlager der Firma Mc. Millan entfernt, in dem wir deutsche Kriegsgefangene wußten.

Luckily, the trapper himself was quite chatty, apparently because he seldom had the opportunity to engage in conversation.

So we soon learned everything worth knowing about the land between Athabasca and Peace River, a town a few hundred miles farther north.

"Well, boys, I believe we will see each other again soon," said the trapper, as he dropped us off at a back road toward evening, and made a telling face.

"What indeed had he meant with these words of farewell," I remarked after awhile, as we had already marched a good bit into the woods.

"And this strange expression in his eyes, as if he ..."

Heinz spoke no further, and we each kept our own thoughts; but an unpleasant feeling crept over me whenever I thought of the trapper.

We made good progress on our way since a snow plow had cleared the snow; as twilight set in we were about two hours away from the lumberjack camp of the Mc. Millan Company, which we knew housed German prisoners of war.

III

Das Holzfällerlager am Fawcettlake

Der Fawcettlake ist einer jener vielen tausend Seen, die überall in den riesigen Waldgebieten Nordkanadas eingestreut liegen.

An seinem Nordende befinden sich einige Blockhäuser und eine Sägemühle.

Während des Krieges wurden deutsche Kriegsgefangene in starkem Maße in der Holzindustrie Kanadas eingesetzt,

und so befanden sich auch seit etlichen Jahren im Fawcettsee-Lager etwa 40 deutsche Kriegsgefangene, die teils als Holzfäller, teils in der Sägemühle beschäftigt waren.

Der Mond stand schon hoch am Himmel, als wir uns dem Lager näherten.

The lumberjack camp at Fawcett Lake

Fawcett Lake is one of those many thousands of lakes that are interspersed all over the huge forested areas of Northern Canada.

At its Northern end, there were a few log houses and a saw mill.

During the war, large numbers of German prisoners of war were used in the Canadian lumber industry,

and so about 40 German POWs found themselves in Fawcett Lake Camp for several years, some of them worked as lumberjacks, others in the sawmill.

The moon was already high in the sky when we were approaching the camp.

17

Verträumt lagen die Hütten im Schnee, friedlicher Lichtschein drang aus den Fenstern …

und wie wir dastanden und lauschten, trug uns der Nachtwind die schwachen Klänge einer Mandoline zu – „Heimatland, Heimatland!" – weit von der deutschen Heimat entfernt drang diese Melodie in die klare Märznacht Kanadas.

„Wenn es uns gelingt, unbemerkt in jene Hütte zu kommen, dann sind wir für die nächsten Wochen vor der Polizei sicher", flüsterte Heinz.

„Ja, die halten bestimmt dicht; ich möchte nur wissen, wie es hier draußen mit der Bewachung ist", entgegnete ich.

Langsam pirschten wir uns näher an das Lager heran; es lag so still und friedlich da, alles schien in den Hütten zu sein – da, plötzlich schlägt ein Hund an, eine Taschenlampe blitzt auf, Schritte nähern sich.

Mit einigen Sätzen sind wir seitwärts hinter einem Holzstapel verschwunden, kriechen im tiefen Schnee weiter – nur jetzt nicht geschnappt werden!

Als wir für einen Augenblick verschnauften, war alles ruhig.

Wir umschlichen das Lager, versuchten es von der anderen Seite.

Dreamily the huts lay in the snow, peaceful light glowed through the windows …

and, as we stood and listened, the night wind carried the faint sounds of a mandolin to us – "Heimatland, Heimatland!" – far away from the German homeland, this melody streamed out into the clear Canadian March night.

"If we manage to slip into this hut unnoticed, then we'll be safe from the police for the next few weeks," whispered Heinz.

"Yes, I'm sure they'll keep the secret; I just want to know what's up out here with the guards," I replied.

Slowly we prowled toward the camp; it lay so peaceful and quiet, everyone seemed to be in the huts – there, suddenly a dog was alarmed, a flashlight lit up, footsteps approached.

With a few leaps, we disappeared sideways behind a pile of wood, crawling farther through the deep snow – just don't get caught now!

As we caught our breath for a moment, everything was silent.

We crept around the camp, tried it from the other side.

Eine Hütte lag ganz zwischen den Bäumen.

One hut lay right between the trees.

Mit angehaltenem Atem näherten wir uns dem Fenster.

With bated breath we neared the window.

Wir erblickten einige Männer in Holzfällerkleidung um einen Tisch sitzend und sich unterhaltend.

We spotted some men in lumberjack clothes sitting around a table and talking.

Verstehen konnten wir nichts – schade.

We couldn't understand anything – too bad.

„Wenn wir nur wüßten, ob es kanadische Zivilarbeiter oder deutsche Kriegsgefangene sind", raunte ich Heinz zu.

"If only we knew whether they are Canadian workers or German POWs," I murmured to Heinz.

Vorsichtig schlichen wir zur nächsten Hütte.

Carefully we crept to the next hut.

Plötzlich geht die Tür auf, ein Mann tritt heraus und erblickt uns im vollen, herausflutenden Lichtschein.

Suddenly the door opened, a man stepped outside and spotted us in the full light flooding out from the hut.

„Nanu, was wollt ihr denn hier?" spricht er uns auf deutsch an.

"Nanu, was wollt ihr denn hier?" – "Hey, what do you want here?" he addressed us in German.

Fast wären wir ihm um den Hals gefallen.

We almost hugged him.

Schnell traten wir in die Hütte, zogen den Mann hinter uns hinein und schlossen die Tür.

We quickly entered the hut, pulled the man inside behind us and closed the door.

„Gott sei Dank – also ihr seid doch deutsche Kriegsgefangene", stieß ich hastig hervor.

"Thank God – so you are in fact German POWs," I said hastily.

„Na klar, was denn sonst?

"Of course, what else?

Und wer seid ihr?"

And who are you?"

„Dasselbe.

Durchgegangen von Wainwright und seit zwei Tagen unterwegs."

„Großartig.

Anständige Entfernung bis hierher; wie habt ihr das so schnell geschafft?"

„Gehitchhiked, hatten viel Glück; und wollten hier gern ein paar Wochen unterschlupfen, bis die ärgste Polizeisuche vorbei ist; wird das gehen?"

„Selbstredend; gleich kommt der Lagerführer; ein prima Kerl, mit dem müßt ihr das Nähere besprechen."

Da trat er schon ein.

Schnell orientierten wir ihn über uns und unsere Absichten.

„Geht in Ordnung, heute nacht bleibt ihr mal im Waschhaus, morgen sehen wir weiter.

Und jetzt schnell, denn um 11 ist Zählung – unser Sergeant ist ziemlich genau, gleich wird er kommen."

Schon wurden wir in die nächste Hütte, das Waschhaus, geleitet.

„Aber ihr seid ja völlig durchnäßt.

Wartet, gleich komme ich wieder."

"The same.

Escaped from Wainwright and on the run for two days."

"Magnificent.

That's a fair distance to here; how did you make it so quickly?"

"Hitchhiked, had lots of luck; and would like to take cover here for a few weeks, until the worst of the police search is over; would that be ok?"

"Of course; the camp leader will come soon; a great guy, you'll have to discuss the details with him."

At that moment, he entered.

Quickly we informed him about us and our intentions.

"That's fine, tonight you can stay in the wash house, tomorrow we'll consider further.

And now hurry, because there's a count at 11 – our sergeant is very precise, he will come soon."

We were guided to the next hut, the wash house.

"You guys are completely soaked.

Wait, I'll be right back."

Und nach wenigen Minuten erhielten wir trockene Kleider und hängten unser nasses Zeug an den warmen Ofen.

Inzwischen war Zählung in den Hütten; kaum war sie beendet, da huschten ein paar Gestalten zum Waschhaus, brachten zu essen und zu trinken – und dann saßen wir noch lange beisammen, und das Erzählen nahm kein Ende.

„Da habt ihr wirklich Schwein gehabt, daß ihr nicht in die erste Hütte hineingingt – da wohnen nämlich kanadische Zivilarbeiter;

und wenn erst einer von euch weiß, dann ist es im Nu herum – bei den wenigen Neuigkeiten hier oben", meinte er.

„Und was habt ihr weiter vor, wenn die Suchaktion der Polizei nachgelassen hat?" fragte ein anderer.

„Zunächst in die Staaten und Geld verdienen; und dann an die Ostküste in einen der Häfen, wo täglich Schiffe nach Europa abgehen.

Sind wir aber erst in Europa, dann wird sich ein Weg nach Deutschland finden lassen."

Es war lange nach Mitternacht, als wir uns endlich zur Ruhe legten.

After just a few minutes we had dry clothing and were hanging our wet stuff over the warm stove.

Meanwhile the count was going on in the huts; as soon as it was over a few figures scurried over to the wash house bringing food and drinks – and then we sat together for quite awhile, and the story telling wouldn't come to an end.

"You were quite lucky not to enter the first hut – because Canadian workers live there;

and if one of them knew about you, then it would have been over in a moment – with the news being very sparse up here," he said.

"And what are your plans once the police search has ceased?" asked another.

"At first to the States and earn some money; and then to the East Coast to one of the port cities where ships depart daily to Europe.

Once we're in Europe, we'll find a way to get to Germany."

It was long after midnight when we finally lay down to rest.

Man ist uns auf der Spur

„Aufstehen! Kommt schnell mit rüber!"

Der Lagerführer selbst war es, der uns weckte.

Schlaftrunken folgten wir ihm durch die Dunkelheit.

Wir betraten eine andere Hütte, die größer war als die übrigen.

„Hier hinauf!"

Der Lagerführer weist mit der Hand nach oben auf eine Luke in der Decke neben dem Ofenrohr.

Wir bestiegen den Tisch, einen Schemel und zwängten uns durch die Öffnung.

Ein paar Decken und ein Korb mit Fressalien wurden uns nachgeschoben.

„Alles andere später", hörten wir den Lagerführer noch rufen, und schon wurde die Luke zugeschoben.

Wir waren allein; nur undeutlich drangen einige Geräusche von draußen zu uns.

Allem Anschein nach ging es bereits zur Arbeit, obgleich es noch völlig dunkel war, sicher hatten sie einen weiten Weg zur Arbeitsstelle.

They're on our trail

"Get up! Come with us quickly, over there!"

It was the camp leader himself who woke us.

Drowsy, we followed him through the darkness.

We entered a different hut, which was bigger than all the others.

"Up here!"

The camp leader pointed upwards with his hand to a hatch in the ceiling next to the stovepipe.

We climbed on the table and a footstool and squeezed ourselves through the opening.

A few blankets and a basket with grub were shoved after us.

"Everything else later," we heard the camp leader call, and the hatch was already being closed.

We were alone; only a few faint noises reached us from outside.

In all likelihood work was already starting, even though it was still completely dark, surely they had a long way to their workplace.

Langsam rannen die Stunden; es wurde heiß und stickig um uns; trotzdem schliefen wir ein.

The hours passed by slowly; it became hot and stuffy all around us; nevertheless we fell asleep.

Als wir aufwachten, waren wir in Schweiß gebadet.

When we woke up, we were soaked in sweat.

Schritte wurden hörbar, die Luke wurde aufgeschoben.

Steps could be heard, the hatch was being pulled open.

„Dicke Luft", raunte uns jemand zu.

"Trouble's brewing," somebody murmured to us.

Wir schauten hinab und erblickten den Lagerführer.

We looked down and spotted the camp leader.

„Im Radio wurde soeben euer Steckbrief durchgegeben."

"Your escape bulletin has just been announced on the radio."

„Nun, das hatten wir ja erwartet."

"Well, we expected that."

„Gewiß", meinte er, „aber es wurde dazu gesagt, daß ihr euch hier in den Wäldern herumtreiben müßtet, denn ein Trapper hätte zwei verdächtige Leute, auf die die Beschreibung paßt, ein Stück des Wegs mitgenommen.

"Sure," he said, "but it was also said that you must be lingering out here in the woods, because a trapper gave two suspicious people, who fit the description, a ride along part of the way.

„Verdammt kitzlige Geschichte."

"Damn ticklish story."

„Das beste, ihr verschwindet so bald als möglich aus dem Lager.

"It would be best if you leave the camp as soon as possible.

Ich habe schon einen genauen Plan für euch", und dann begann der Lagerführer uns seine bis in alle Einzelheiten getroffenen Vorbereitungen zu schildern.

I already have a specific plan for you," and then the camp leader began to describe to us in great detail all of the preparations he had made.

Wenige Stunden später verließen wir unser Versteck.

Wir hatten Buschkleidung an und Holzfällermützen auf dem Kopf.

Auf dem Rücken trugen wir Äxte.

Zwei scheinbar zufällig daherkommende Kriegsgefangene gesellten sich zu uns und begleiteten uns in den Wald.

Unter Fichtenzweigen versteckt tief aus dem Schnee zogen sie zwei Säcke hervor, luden sie uns auf den Buckel, drückten uns eine Wegskizze in die Hand, gaben uns noch ein paar Verhaltungsmaßregeln, wünschten uns Glück und entfernten sich rasch wieder zum Lager.

Wir waren allein.

A few hours later we left our hideout.

We were wearing local clothing and lumberjack hats on our heads.

On our backs we carried axes.

Two prisoners of war, who seemed to come at random, joined us and accompanied us into the forest.

From deep in the snow under some spruce branches, they pulled out two sacks, loaded them on our backs, pressed a sketched map into our hands, gave us a few more rules of conduct, wished us luck and quickly headed back to the camp.

We were alone.

IV

Allein in der Wildnis

Nachdem wir etwa zwei Stunden auf dem uns bezeichneten Holzabfuhrweg entlangmarschiert waren, mochten wir jene Stelle erreicht haben, an der linker Hand etwa 3,5 km entfernt eine seit mehreren Jahren verlassene Waldschmiede liegen sollte, die wir als Unterschlupf für die nächsten Wochen benutzen wollten.

Wir waren auf unserem Weg immer tiefer in den Wald hineingelangt und spähten nun eifrig nach einer halbwegs gangbaren Abzweigung, doch undurchdringlich stand die Wand des Waldes, hohe Schneemassen türmten sich zu beiden Seiten des Weges.

Schließlich gelangten wir an einen quer über den Weg gestürzten Urwaldriesen.

„Den benutzen wir, um unsere Spuren zu verwischen", meinte Heinz.

Alone in the wilderness

After we were marching for about two hours along the indicated logging road, we might have reached the spot, on the left hand side about 3.5 Kilometers away, where the long abandoned forge should be, that we wanted to use as shelter for the next few weeks.

We were going along the path ever deeper into the forest and scouted eagerly for a reasonably passable junction, but the wall of forest stood impenetrable, high snow banks piled up on either side of the path.

Eventually we reached a giant tree that had fallen across the path.

"Let's use this one to cover our tracks," suggested Heinz.

Wir gingen noch ein paar hundert Meter weiter, dann rückwärts in unseren eigenen Spuren zurück,

bestiegen den Baum, balancierten auf ihm entlang und landeten schließlich etwa 35 m abseits vom Wege im hohen Schnee zwischen Brombeergebüsch und Fichtenjungwuchs.

Der Schnee reichte uns bis über die Hüften, aber unverzagt begannen wir, uns einen Weg in Richtung der gesuchten Waldschmiede zu bahnen.

Nach etwa 100 m waren wir bereits so erschöpft, daß uns klar wurde, daß wir in dieser Nacht unser Ziel nicht mehr erreichen würden;

unser schweres Gepäck zog uns vollends nieder, und mit dem Ruf: „Hier laßt uns Hütten bauen", warf ich es ab.

Was hatte uns der gute Lagerführer auch alles mitgegeben; nichts war vergessen worden:

Verpflegung für eine Woche, acht Decken, warmes Unterzeug, Kochgeschirr, eine Schaufel und Werkzeug – kurz alles, was man zum Leben in der Wildnis braucht.

Schnell war der Schnee beiseite geschaufelt, eine Fichte gefällt, Holz gespalten und ein Feuer entzündet.

Bald kochte das Kaffeewasser im Topf, brutzelten Eier und Zwiebeln in der Pfanne und briet der Speck.

We continued a few hundred meters farther, then reversed back in our own tracks,

climbed onto the tree, balanced along it and finally landed about 35 meters away from the path in deep snow between blackberry bushes and spruce saplings.

The snow level reached all the way up above our hips, but we nonetheless began cutting a trail toward the sought-after forge.

After about 100 meters we were already so worn out that we realized we wouldn't reach our target that night;

our heavy packs were dragging us down, and with the call: "Let's build shelter here," I threw it off.

The kind camp leader had supplied us with everything; nothing had been forgotten:

food for a week, eight blankets, thermal underwear, cooking gear, a shovel and tools – in short, everything one needs to survive in the wilderness.

We quickly shoveled snow out of the way, fell a spruce, split wood and lit a fire.

Soon water for coffee was boiling in the pot, eggs and onions were frying in the pan along with bacon.

Mit viel Geschick bereitete Heinz unterdessen ein weiches Lager aus Fichtenzweigen – und dann saßen wir nieder und verzehrten unser erstes Urwaldmahl, während unsere durchnäßten Kleider am Feuer hingen und ihre Feuchtigkeit ausdampften.

Dann legten wir uns nieder, warm von Decken umhüllt und zusätzlich vom Feuer angestrahlt.

Zwischen den langsam hin und her wiegenden Wipfeln schaute der gestirnte Himmel auf uns herab.

Wir waren zufrieden und glücklich.

Plötzlich fuhren wir hoch.

Ganz in unserer Nähe ertönte ein langgezogenes Heulen, dann noch eins etwas weiter links und ein drittes in unserem Rücken – Wölfe!

Eine Gänsehaut lief uns über den Rücken, alle Wolfsgeschichten, die wir gelesen hatten, fielen uns ein, unwillkürlich griffen wir nach den Äxten.

Es war ein unheimliches Gefühl – noch fehlte uns jegliche Erfahrung; wir legten einige Scheite aufs Feuer und rückten unsere Eßvorräte ganz nahe an uns heran.

Das Feuer hielt die Wölfe in erträglicher Entfernung, näher als 50 m kamen sie wohl niemals heran.

With great skill Heinz prepared a soft bed out of spruce branches – and then we sat down and ate our first wilderness meal, while our soaked clothing hung next to the fire, the moisture evaporating.

Then we lay down, warm from the surrounding blankets and the heat from the fire.

Between the branches that swayed back and forth, the star-filled sky looked down at us.

We were content and happy.

Suddenly we sprung up.

Very close by, a long howl bellowed out along with another a little bit farther left and yet a third behind our backs – wolves!

Goose bumps spread down our backs as all the wolf tales we had read came back to us, we involuntarily reached for the axes.

It was a scary feeling – having had no experience with such a thing; we put a few pieces of wood onto the fire and moved our food very close to us.

The fire kept the wolves at a reasonable distance, they probably never got closer than 50 meters.

Allmählich beruhigten wir uns wieder, auch machten sich die Anstrengungen der letzten Tage bemerkbar und schließlich fielen wir in einen festen, traumlosen Schlaf.

Gradually we relaxed again, also the labors of the previous days began to be noticed and we finally fell into a deep, dreamless sleep.

Die Sonne stand schon hoch am Himmel, als wir am anderen Tage mit etwas steif gefrorenen Gliedern erwachten.

The sun was standing high in the sky when we awoke the next day with somewhat stiff, frozen limbs.

Rasch wurde das Feuer in Gang gebracht und Kaffee gebraut.

Quickly the fire was revived and coffee brewed.

Nach dem Frühstück brachen wir unverzüglich auf.

After breakfast we set out without delay.

Wieder balancierten wir über einen umgestürzten Baum, um unsere Spuren erneut zu verschleiern.

Again we balanced across a fallen-over tree to cover our tracks anew.

Unter unglaublichen Anstrengungen bahnten wir uns unseren Weg durch die Schneemassen.

With unbelievable exertion we made our way through the snowbanks.

Immer häufiger fielen wir hin, wenn wir uns in den unter der Schneedecke verborgenen Brombeerranken verhedderten,

Ever more frequently we fell down, when we became entangled in the blackberry bushes hidden under the layers of snow,

immer öfter mußten wir Ruhepausen einlegen

ever more often we had to take a rest break

– und nach vier Stunden waren wir so erschöpft, daß wir nicht mehr weiter konnten.

– and after four hours we were so exhausted, that we could no longer go farther.

Wir mochten etwa zwei Kilometer zurückgelegt haben und versuchten nach einer kräftigenden Mahlzeit die Waldschmiede zunächst ohne unser Gepäck aufzufinden.

We had probably hiked about two kilometers and after a hearty meal we first tried to find the forge without our packs.

Dabei gerieten wir in einen Windbruch, aus dem wir schier nicht mehr hinauskamen.

Wie Streichhölzer geknickt lagen die gewaltigen Fichten und Pappeln übereinander, hoch ragten Wurzelenden in die Luft, kahl und gespenstig standen einige zersplitterte Stämme dazwischen.

„Welch ein Holzreichtum!"

„Und niemand, der es abfährt und verwertet!

In zehn Jahren wird dieser Windbruch von Jungwuchs überwuchert sein, die Stämme werden vermodern und nachfolgenden Baumgenerationen als Nährstoff dienen …"

Es dämmerte bereits, als wir unseren Rastplatz wieder erreicht hatten.

Schnell hatten wir ein Lager errichtet, legten uns nieder und waren sofort eingeschlafen.

Schon in aller Frühe des nächsten Tages brachen wir auf, um uns an einem verabredeten Punkt mit dem Lagerführer zu treffen.

Bei dieser Gelegenheit wollten wir die näheren Einzelheiten des Verpflegungsnachschubes und dergleichen besprechen.

Hinter einer großen Fichte versteckt lagen wir auf der Lauer, den Treffpunkt in unserem Blickfeld.

In the process, we were caught in a slashing wind from which we barely escaped.

Like broken matches, huge spruce and cottonwood trees were lying on top of each other, roots pointing high into the air with a few splintered stumps in between, stark and spooky.

"What a wealth of lumber!"

"And nobody to haul it away and use it!

In ten years this fallen lumber will be overgrown by young trees, the stumps will rot and provide the new generations of trees with a nutrition base …"

Day was already dawning as we reached our resting place again.

Quickly we had built a camp, laid ourselves down and were instantly asleep.

We set out quite early the next day, in order to meet at a previously arranged spot with the camp leader.

We wanted to use this opportunity to talk about the details of our food supply and such.

Hidden behind a huge spruce, we were lying in wait, our meeting place in sight.

Nachdem wir eine Stunde vergeblich gewartet hatten, erblickten wir endlich eine sich vorsichtig heranpirschende Gestalt – es war nicht der Lagerführer.

After we had waited in vain for an hour, we finally spotted a cautiously approaching figure – it was not the camp leader.

Schließlich erkannten wir einen unserer Helfer, der uns aus dem Lager hinausbegleitet hatte.

Finally we recognized one of our helpers, who had accompanied us out of the camp.

Wir gaben uns zu erkennen.

We revealed ourselves.

Hastig zog er einen Zettel aus der Tasche, drückte uns das Papier in die Hand und verschwand eilends wieder.

Hastily he pulled a note out of his pocket, pressed the paper into our hands and disappeared again in a hurry.

Mit zitternden Händen entfalteten wir den Brief und lasen folgende Botschaft:

With shaking hands we unfolded the letter and read the following message:

„Eine Viertelstunde nach Eurem Abmarsch erschien die Polizei im Lager,

"A quarter of an hour after your departure the police appeared in camp,

durchsuchte alle Räume und möglichen Verstecke einschließlich des Dachbodens, nahm nach einer mitgebrachten Kartei einen Bildvergleich mit allen Lagerangehörigen vor, kontrollierte die Küchenvorräte und stellte sie unter strengste Bewachung.

searched all the rooms and possible hideouts including the attic, compared every camp member to a file photo they brought, checked the food supplies and placed them under the strictest surveillance.

Ich selbst werde ständig von einem Polizisten begleitet, alle meine Handlungen werden bewacht; seit gestern ist eine kleine Polizeifunkstation im Lager.

I myself am constantly escorted by a policeman, all of my actions are guarded; since yesterday there's been a small police radio station in the camp.

Indianer und Trapper mit Hundeschlitten suchen das Gelände nach euch ab.

Indians and trappers with dog sleds are searching the area for you.

Sucht nicht die Waldschmiede auf, sondern bleibt auf engstem Raum.

Do not go to the forge in the woods, but stay in close range.

Wegen Rauchentwicklung möglichst kein Feuer am Tage anzünden.

Verpflegungsnachschub völlig ausgeschlossen.

Wenn eure Vorräte aufgebraucht sind, versucht im PW-Lager Chisholm, 70 km südlich von hier am Athabaska-river gelegen, unterzuschlüpfen.

Hals- und Beinbruch!"

„Schöne Bescherung!

– Hoffentlich entstehen dem Lager keine Nachteile durch uns", sagte Heinz schließlich, als wir die Nachrichten etwas verdaut hatten.

„Mit unseren Vorräten kommen wir noch 6 Tage aus – und dann marschieren wir eben los.

Hier wird uns jedenfalls so leicht keiner finden."

Bald waren wir wieder an unserem Lagerplatz angelangt.

Er erschien uns aber doch etwas zu nahe am Holzabfuhrweg gelegen und wir beschlossen, noch tiefer in den Wald zu gehen.

Lederstrumpf hätte die Verschleierung seiner Spuren kaum besser einleiten können.

Because of smoke, do not light a fire during the day if possible.

Replenishing food is completely impossible.

Once your supplies have been used up, try to slip into POW Camp Chisholm, located 70 Kilometers south of here on the Athabasca River.

Break a leg!"

"What a mess!

– Hopefully the camp didn't suffer any consequences because of us," said Heinz finally, when we had digested the news a bit.

"With our supplies we can manage another 6 days – and then we will start marching.

Here, anyway, no one will find us easily."

Soon we had arrived back at our camp.

It appeared to us however to be located too close to the logging road and we decided to go even deeper into the woods.

Leatherstocking could hardly have done better at covering his tracks.

Mit einer gefährlichen Kletterpartie über mehrere ineinandergestürzte Bäume begann sie, dann benutzten wir eine Elchspur, dann wieder Bäume, und erst mehrere Meter weiter hinterließen wir wieder unsere eigenen Spuren.

It began with a dangerous climb across multiple fallen trees, then we used moose tracks, then trees again, and only a few meters farther we started leaving our own tracks again.

Nach einer Stunde fanden wir einen Platz, der uns sicher erschien und für die Errichtung eines Lagers geeignet.

After an hour we found a spot that seemed safe, and fit for setting up a camp.

Wir bauen eine Blockhütte

We build a log hut

Die folgenden sechs Tage Urwaldleben werden uns immer unvergeßlich bleiben.

The following six days of wilderness life will always remain unforgettable.

Mit Feuereifer machten wir uns sogleich an die Errichtung einer kleinen Blockhütte.

With zeal we applied ourselves at once to the construction of a small log hut.

Nach zwei Tagen war sie im Wesentlichen fertig.

After two days it was basically finished.

Dann gingen wir an die Ausgestaltung des Vorplatzes, zimmerten bequeme Sitzgelegenheiten und einen Tisch und schufen allmählich alle Voraussetzungen für ein behagliches Dasein.

Then we proceeded to arrange the outside area, built comfortable seats and a table, and gradually created all the necessities for a cozy existence.

Wir durften uns nun auch recht sicher fühlen, denn es hatte gleich in der ersten Nacht geschneit und von unseren Spuren war nichts mehr zu sehen.

We allowed ourselves to feel rather safe now, because it had snowed that first night and there was nothing more to be seen of our tracks.

V

Der Plan mit dem U-Boot

„Wie war das eigentlich bei deinem ersten Fluchtversuch?" fragte mich Heinz eines Abends, „es wurde gemunkelt, du wolltest dich von einem U-Boot abholen lassen."

„Ja, das mit dem U-Boot stimmt schon; ich, d.h. wir, denn wir waren zu viert, hatten damals nicht so viel Glück, wie wir beide heute:

Es war im Sommer 43.

Wir lagen damals in einem Lager im Staate Quebec in Ostkanada.

Unter großen Schwierigkeiten und mit viel Geduld war es uns gelungen, mittels eines Geheim-Codes Verbindung mit der Heimat aufzunehmen.

The plan with the submarine

"So how was it actually on your first escape attempt?" Heinz asked me one evening, "it was rumored that you wanted to get picked up by a submarine."

"Yes, the thing with the submarine is true; I, that is, we, since there were four of us, didn't have as much luck back then as the two of us today:

It was in the summer of '43.

We were stationed at a camp in the province of Quebec in Eastern Canada.

With great difficulty and lots of patience we succeeded in making contact with home using a secret code.

Zu einem festgesetzten Zeitpunkt sollte an einem vereinbarten Ort an der Ostküste der Vereinigten Staaten ein U-Boot auf uns warten, um uns aufzunehmen.

Aber wir hatten die Rechnung ohne die Engländer gemacht.

Die hatten nämlich schon frühzeitig unseren Code dechiffriert und lasen alle hin- und hergehenden Nachrichten mit, ohne es uns merken zu lassen.

Auf diese Weise gedachten sie gleich zwei Fliegen mit einer Klappe zu schlagen, das U-Boot und uns."

„Eine ziemliche Verantwortung, die ihr da auf euch geladen hattet", unterbrach mich Heinz.

„Gewiß, aber Dönitz selbst hatte sich für unseren Vorschlag entschieden, weil er daran interessiert war, aus dem Munde von in Gefangenschaft geratenen U-Boot-Offizieren etwas über die englische U-Boot-Abwehr zu erfahren.

Entsprechende Nachrichten sollten durch uns der Luftwaffenführung zugeleitet werden.

– Aber nun hör weiter:

Wir ahnten also nichts von den Vorbereitungen, die der kanadische Lagerkommandant getroffen hatte, um uns auch sicher zu ergreifen.

At a specified time and an agreed upon location on the East Coast of the United States, a submarine would wait to pick us up.

But we hadn't taken the Brits into account.

Namely, they had long ago deciphered our code and read every message going back and forth, without letting us find out.

This way they thought they'd kill two birds with one stone, the submarine and us."

"Quite a responsibility you had resting on your shoulders there," Heinz interrupted me.

"Sure, but Dönitz himself decided on our plan, because he was interested in learning, directly from the mouths of captured submarine officers, some of their experience with the English submarine defense.

Corresponding messages were to be sent to the air force command through us.

– But now listen further:

We suspected nothing about the preparations that the Canadian camp commander had made, to be certain to capture us.

Im Lager selbst konnte er uns noch nicht fassen, denn er wußte ja nicht, wer von der internen deutschen Lagerführung für das Unternehmen ausersehen war; deshalb verstärkte er in dem fraglichen Zeitraum die Außenbewachung.

He couldn't catch us in the camp itself, since he didn't know who from the internal German camp command had been chosen for this endeavor; therefore he strengthened the outside security for the time period in question.

Daß wir zu viert in jener Augustnacht überhaupt unentdeckt durch die drei Zäune gelangten, ist wohl nur dem fürchterlichen Gewitter zuzuschreiben, das wie bestellt hereinbrach.

That four of us made it through the three fences unnoticed on that August night is indeed only attributed to the fearsome thunderstorm that broke out, as if by request.

Es donnerte unentwegt und goß in Strömen.

It thundered incessantly and poured in sheets.

So hatten wir verhältnismäßig schnell die Lagerumzäunungen überwunden und glaubten uns einigermaßen sicher

So, relatively quickly we overcame the camp fences and believed we were fairly safe

– da blitzten plötzlich Taschenlampen vor uns auf,

– when flashlights suddenly lit up in front of us,

– wir sprangen zur Seite, suchten Deckung hinter ein paar Bäumen, ein Schuß krachte, Schreiber faßte sich an die Brust, von drei Seiten stürzten Wachposten auf uns zu, ergriffen uns und führten uns ab."

– we jumped sideways, sought cover behind a few trees, a shot was fired, Schreiber reached for his chest, guards rushed us from three different directions, captured us and led us away."

„War Schreiber ernstlich verletzt?" fragte Heinz dazwischen.

"Was Schreiber's injury serious?" asked Heinz at that point.

„Er hatte unglaubliches Glück; weißt du, wir hatten uns für den Ausbruch extra Tarnanzüge aus grünen Matratzenschonern geschneidert und vorne mit Reißverschlüssen, die wir von unseren Fliegerstiefeln hatten, versehen.

"He was really lucky; you know, for the escape we had sewn extra camouflage suits out of green mattress covers and equipped in the front with zippers, that we had from our pilot boots.

Die Kugel, die im stumpfen Winkel auf Schreiber abgefeuert wurde, traf genau den Reißverschluß und – prallte ab.

The bullet, which was fired at Schreiber from an obtuse angle, hit directly on the zipper and – deflected off.

Wir wurden dann gleich in Arrestzellen gesperrt und mußten alles, was wir anhatten und besaßen, abgeben.

We were then immediately locked in a detention cell and had to hand over what we were wearing and carrying.

Dabei gelang es mir aber doch noch mein Taschenmesser unter der Pritsche verschwinden zu lassen.

But in the process, I managed to make my pocket knife disappear under a pallet.

Nach einigen Stunden wurden uns trockene Klamotten gebracht, wir wurden in Autos geführt, und los ging die Fahrt.

After a few hours, dry clothes were brought to us, we were put into cars, and the ride began.

Was hatte man mit uns vor?

What were we in for?

Noch nie waren in Kanada bei einem Fluchtversuch ergriffene Kriegsgefangene bei Nacht und Nebel mit abgeblendeten Lichtern aus dem Lager, zu dem sie gehörten, gebracht worden.

Never before in Canada had prisoners of war that were caught trying to escape been taken so stealthily with dimmed lights out of the camp to which they belonged.

Wir hatten beim Einsteigen in die Fahrzeuge keinen Laut von uns geben dürfen, alle Maßnahmen zielten darauf hin, dem Lager unseren Abtransport zu verheimlichen.

While getting into the cars we were not allowed to make any noise, all measures were aimed toward keeping our departure from the camp secret.

Und dann fuhren wir mehrere Stunden durch die Nacht, keiner der mit uns fahrenden Wachposten sprach ein Wort – uns war recht beklommen zu Mute.

And then we rode for several hours through the night, none of the guards that rode with us said a word – we were struck mute with anxiety.

Im Morgengrauen kamen wir in ein leerstehendes P/W-Lager etwa 60 km östlich von unserem Lager.

At daybreak we arrived at an empty P/W camp about 60 kilometers east of our camp.

In the confinement hut the cells were ready for us, and soon the doors were shut behind us.

Naturally we didn't suspect why we were guarded with such care – we only noticed this much: we should, under no circumstances, have contact with our original camp.

That all of our belongings there were being searched in the hope of finding out more about our secret connections with the homeland, never occurred to us,

as we regarded our fast recapture as only bad luck.

Only much later did it become clear to us, that the secret code had been deciphered long before that."

"Did they also catch the submarine?"

"No, luckily they smelled the trap in time and were able to get away from the destroyers that were lying in wait.

I only learned that recently from a naval officer captured not long ago."

VI

Erneut ausgebrochen

„Wie ist es euch dann weiter ergangen?"

„Unser Arrestlokal war eine einzelstehende Holzbarracke.

Draußen patroullierten ständig zwei Wachposten und drinnen einer.

Die Zellen waren völlig leer; wir erhielten nur eine Decke, die wir zum Schlafen auf den Boden breiteten.

Eine Stunde pro Tag wurden wir hinausgeführt und durften unter Bewachung in einem Umkreis von 50 m Spazierengehen.

Dabei konnte ich mir ein gutes Bild von der näheren Umgebung machen und faßte den Entschluß, nochmals auszubrechen.

Ich hatte mein Taschenmesser und Zeit, viel Zeit!

Mehr brauchte ich nicht.

Escaped anew

"What happened to all of you after that?"

"Our confinement hut was a single wooden barrack.

At all times, two guards patrolled outside and one inside.

The cells were completely empty; we were only given a blanket, which we spread on the floor for sleeping.

One hour per day we were led outside and allowed to roam under supervision within a radius of 50 meters.

In the process I got a good picture of the nearby surroundings and made the decision to escape again.

I had my pocket knife and time, lots of time!

I needed no more.

41

Nach drei Tagen hatte ich einige der oberen Dielenbretter vorsichtig aus dem Fußboden herausgelöst, nach zwei weiteren auch die unteren.

Wenn ich die Zelle verließ, fügte ich sie stets sorgsam an ihren Ort – und so blieb der Ausstieg in den Keller unbemerkt.

In der sechsten Nacht stieg ich in den Keller, kroch an eine offenstehende Luke an der Stirnseite und beobachtete die zu beiden Seiten der Baracke auf und ab patrouillierenden Posten.

Endlich waren sie einmal gleichzeitig am Wendepunkt; sie drehten um und schickten sich an, die 10 bis 15 Schritt zurückzugehen.

Auf diesen Moment hatte ich gewartet.

Schnell schob ich mich durch die Öffnung, huschte auf Socken, die Schuhe in der Hand, bis zur nächsten Baracke und warf mich nieder.

Schon wendeten die Posten wieder, kamen Schritt für Schritt zurück.

Immer näher rückten sie heran.

Wenige Schritte neben mir blieben sie stehen.

Das Herz schlug mir bis zum Hals; ich wagte kaum zu atmen.

Die müssen dich doch sehen bei dem hellen Mondlicht, sagte ich mir.

Die Sekunden wurden zu Stunden.

Dann knirschte der Kies.

After three days, I had carefully removed some of the top boards from the floor; after two more, the lower ones too.

Whenever I left the cell, I carefully moved them back into their place – and so the exit into the basement remained unnoticed.

On the sixth night, I climbed into the basement, crawled toward an open hatch at the front side and watched the guards patrolling back and forth on both sides of the barrack.

Finally, they were simultaneously at the turning point; they turned around and started to take the 10 or 15 steps back.

I had been waiting for this moment.

Quickly I pushed myself through the opening, scurried to the next barrack in my socks, with shoes in hand, and threw myself down.

The guards turned around again, coming back step by step.

Ever closer they moved.

A few steps away from me they stopped.

My heart pounded in my throat; I hardly dared to breathe.

They certainly must see you in the bright moonlight, I told myself.

The seconds turned into hours.

Then the gravel crunched.

Jetzt kommt er auf dich zu, und alles ist wieder vergeblich gewesen – dachte ich – aber dann setzten sich die Posten wieder ruhig in Bewegung; auf und ab, auf und ab.

Jedesmal, wenn sie von mir weggingen, schob ich mich um einige Meter weiter, bis ich endlich hinter die nächste Baracke gelangte.

Dann hatte ich Deckung, lief am Zaun des leer stehenden Lagers entlang, überstieg ihn an einer geeigneten Stelle und verschwand im Dunkel der Nacht."

„Sag mal", unterbrach Heinz meine Erzählung, „wie hattest du dir eigentlich das Weiterkommen gedacht?

Dir fehlte doch alles, was zum Gelingen der Flucht bis zur Küste notwendig war; du hattest weder Geld noch Ausweis, weder Karten noch Kompaß, und in deiner Kleidung konntest du dich auch nirgends sehen lassen."

„Natürlich war mir klar, daß ich erst einmal zu einer vernünftigen Ausrüstung kommen mußte, und zwar schnell, um das U-Boot noch zu erreichen.

Ich hatte vor, unser Stammlager, aus dem wir ja wegtransportiert worden waren, aufzusuchen und über eine Geheimverbindung, die ich mit einem zurückgebliebenen Kameraden verabredet hatte, mir das Nötige zu beschaffen.

Now he's going to find you and everything will be lost again – I thought – but then the guards were once again in motion; back and forth, back and forth.

Every time, when they turned away from me, I pushed myself along a few meters, until I was finally behind the next barrack.

Then I had cover, ran along the fence of the deserted camp, climbed over at a suitable point and disappeared into the dark of night."

"Tell me," Heinz interrupted my story, "how did you actually think you would proceed?

You were missing everything that was necessary for a successful escape to the coast; you had neither money nor ID, neither maps nor compass, and in those clothes you couldn't risk being seen anywhere."

"Of course, it was clear to me that I must first acquire the proper gear, and quickly, in order to reach the submarine.

I had planned to go back to the main camp from which we had been deported and acquire the necessary things via a secret link I had established with a comrade who stayed behind.

Dieser hatte sich in monatelanger Arbeit auf dem Sportplatz, der nur tags betreten werden durfte, ein Loch gegraben und es mit einem Grasdeckel so geschickt getarnt, daß es nicht auffiel.

Jeden Abend, wenn wir den Sportplatz verließen, nahmen wir ein paar Hosentaschen voll Erde mit und so entstand schließlich ein geräumiger Unterschlupf, groß genug, um eine Person zu verbergen.

Darin wollte er sich dann verstecken, um nach Räumung des Sportplatzes nach Einbruch der Dunkelheit durch den verhältnismäßig schlecht bewachten Zaun des Sportplatzes zu entwischen."

„Du wolltest also nachts in den Sportplatz hineinschleichen und in dem Loch eine entsprechende Nachricht hinterlegen, die er dann am nächsten Tag beim Weitergraben finden mußte."

„Genau das.

Nachdem ich also glücklich aus der Arrestzelle entkommen war und mich außerhalb des Lagers befand, marschierte ich die ganze Nacht hindurch bis zum Morgengrauen in westlicher Richtung.

Außer der Himmelsrichtung hatte ich von der Lage des Lagers nur unklare Vorstellungen.

Mir fehlte ja jede Karte.

This guy had dug a hole, with months of work in the sports field, which was only accessible during the daytime, and had disguised it so well with a grass cover, that it was not noticed.

Every evening, when we left the sports field, we took a few pockets full of soil with us, and so eventually a roomy shelter came into being, big enough to conceal a person.

In there he wanted to hide himself until after the sports field was cleared at dusk, in order to slip away through the relatively poorly guarded fence of the sports field."

"So you wanted to sneak onto the sports field at night and leave a message in the hole that he would find the next day when he continued digging."

"Precisely that.

After I had made my lucky escape from the detention cell and found myself outside the camp, I marched the entire night through until dawn, in a westerly direction.

Aside from the general direction, I had only vague notions of the location of the camp.

I was missing any sort of map.

Straßen wagte ich wegen der zu erwartenden Nachsuche nicht zu benutzen, und so lief ich immer querfeldein, die Sterne als Richtungsweiser benutzend.

I didn't dare use roads because of an expected search, and so I always ran cross-country, using the stars as my guide.

Irgendwann mußte ich mal an den Richelieu-Strom kommen, der aus dem Champlain-See nach Norden in den St. Lorenz fließt, und dahinter, das wußte ich, lag das Lager.

At some point I had to reach the Richelieu River, which flows north from Lake Champlain into the St. Lawrence, and beyond that, I knew, lay the camp.

Wie du weißt, ist die Provinz Quebec im Süden ziemlich dicht besiedelt, fast ausschließlich von Franzosen.

As you know, the southern portion of Quebec province is quite densely populated, almost solely by the French.

Überall liegen kleine Dörfer und ringsherum die Äcker; dazwischen sind Wiesen, Weiden und Gehölze eingestreut, und die gesamte Landschaft macht einen sehr lieblichen Eindruck.

There are small villages everywhere and around them are fields; scattered here and there in between are grasslands, pastures and woods, and the whole landscape makes a very lovely impression.

Als der Morgen graute, suchte ich ein kleines Gehölz auf, bestieg einen Baum und verschaffte mir einen Überblick;

As day broke, I visited a small grove, climbed a tree and got an overview;

weit hinter mir lag das Lager, und bei seinem Anblick überkam mich noch einmal die ganze Freude über den gelungenen Ausbruch;

far behind me lay the camp, and seeing it filled me with joy that I had successfully escaped;

vor mir sah ich eine Hügelkette, die sich nach Süden fortsetzte; es mochten wohl die Green Mountains sein, die im wesentlichen schon zu USA gehören.

in front of me was a ridge that continued into the South; it was probably the Green Mountains, which mainly belong to the USA.

Aus den Dörfern fuhren die ersten Wagen zur Ernte auf die Felder, große, zweirädrige Karren mit schweren Kaltblutpferden davor, wie man sie in Frankreich sieht.

From the villages came the first wagons out onto the fields for the harvest, big two-wheeled carts pulled by heavy draft horses, like those seen in France.

45

Es begann lebhaft auf den Äckern zu werden, und ich suchte mir ein gutes Versteck aus, in dem ich den ganzen Tag schlafend und dösend zubrachte.

Gegen Abend meldete sich der Hunger;

ich fand einige Beeren, auch entdeckte ich einen wilden Apfelbaum und aß die noch unreifen Äpfel mit viel Genuß.

Dann brach ich auf.

Ich kam an einigen Gehöften vorbei, die Farmer saßen mit ihren Familien in der warmen Abendluft davor, ich hörte eine Ziehharmonika, es wurde gesungen und gelacht.

In jenen Augenblicken wurde mir die Geschlossenheit und der kulturelle Zusammenhalt der Franco-Kanadier, die rund ein Drittel der kanadischen Bevölkerung ausmachen, so recht deutlich.

Auf dem Weitermarsch kam ich an einen Wald; ich wollte hindurch, aber es war unmöglich, denn alles war so dicht und verfilzt, daß ich rettungslos hängengeblieben wäre.

So mußte ich einen großen Umweg machen und kam dabei durch eine Ortschaft.

Der Marktplatz war etwas erleuchtet, und als ich an einer Hauswand entlangschlich, blieb ich plötzlich wie angewurzelt stehen, starrte an die Wand …

The fields started to come alive, and I chose a suitable hideout where I spent the whole day, sleeping and dozing.

Toward evening, hunger called;

I found some berries; I also discovered a wild apple tree and ate the still unripe apples with great pleasure.

Then I set out.

I passed by a few homesteads where farmers and their families sat out front in the warm evening air; I heard an accordion accompanied by singing and laughter.

In those moments, I realized so clearly the closeness and the cultural solidarity of the Franco-Canadians, which make up about a third of the Canadian population.

While hiking along, I came to a forest; I wanted to pass through it, but it was impossible because everything was so dense and matted that I would have become hopelessly entangled.

So I had to make a huge detour and in the process went through a small village.

The market place was barely lit and while sneaking along the wall of a building, I stopped suddenly as if rooted to the ground, stared at the wall …

Mein eigenes Bild blickte mich an, darunter stand meine Personalbeschreibung – kalt lief es mir den Rücken herunter;

My own picture looked back at me, underneath was my description – chills ran down my back;

das Gefühl, vor dem eigenen Steckbrief zu stehen, ist nur schwer zu beschreiben; aber ich hatte nicht lange Zeit, meinen Gefühlen nachzuhängen,

the feeling of standing in front of your own wanted poster is quite hard to describe; but I didn't have a long time to dwell on my feelings,

– nur schnell aus diesem Ort hinaus, dachte ich und eilte weiter.

– just quickly get out of this place, I thought and hurried along.

Nazi recherché

L'officier, d'aviation allemand CONRAD KLAUS, qui s'est évadé d'un camp d'internement situé près de la métropole, de bonne heure hier matin. Agé de 27 ans, il mesure 5 pieds, 9 pouces et demi, pèse 155 livres et a les yeux et les cheveux bruns. Une petite verrue à la gorge facilite son identification. Lors de sa fuite, il était vêtu d'un pantalon gris foncé en flanelle, d'une chemise sportive verte et d'une cravate noire. Il ne parle que l'allemand et un peu d'anglais.

Fast hatte ich den Ortsausgang erreicht, nur noch drei Häuser lagen vor mir – da blitzte eine Taschenlampe auf, leuchtete mich an, ich wurde angerufen, zum Stehenbleiben aufgefordert.

I had almost reached the end of the village, only three houses still lay ahead of me – then a flashlight blazed on, lit me up, I was being called, asked to stop.

Jetzt ging alles blitzschnell; mit ein paar Sätzen war ich zwischen den Häusern, sprang über einen niedrigen Gartenzaun, eilte zwischen den Beeten entlang, erreichte das freie Feld und verschwand im Dunkel der Nacht.

Now everything went very quickly; with a few darts I was in between the houses, jumped a low fence, hurried between the garden beds, reached an open field and disappeared into the darkness of night.

Ich vernahm noch mehrmals Rufen hinter mir, sah auch den Lichtkegel der Taschenlampe das Gelände absuchen – aber der Abstand zwischen meinem Verfolger und mir wurde immer größer, und bald hatte er meine Spur verloren.

I still heard multiple calls behind me, also saw the conical beam of the flashlight searching the area – but the distance between my follower and me grew ever larger, and soon he had lost my trail.

Ich kam an einen Bach, watete einige 100 Meter aufwärts, um meine Spuren zu verschleiern, und gelangte an ein großes Maisfeld.

I came to a stream, waded a few hundred meters upstream to conceal my tracks, and arrived at a huge cornfield.

Darin verschnaufte ich endlich und fand zu meiner Überraschung die Kolben schon reif.

There I finally paused for breath and found to my surprise the corncobs already ripe.

Herrlich haben mir die zarten jungen Maiskörner geschmeckt.

The soft, young grains of corn tasted wonderful.

Nach einer Weile näherte ich mich in einem großen Bogen wieder der Straße.

After a while, I approached the road again in a wide arc.

Sie war menschenleer, und ich kam gut vorwärts.

It was deserted, and I made good progress.

Im Morgengrauen schleppte ich einige Garben von einem frisch geschnittenen Kornfeld in ein Gehölz und schlief darin bis zum Abend.

With the break of day I hauled some sheaves from a freshly cut cornfield into a grove and slept there until evening.

Über den Richelieu-Strom

Crossing the Richelieu River

In der dritten Nacht endlich erreichte ich den Strom.

On the third night I finally reached the river.

Ein Versuch, durch den breiten Schilfgürtel ans offene Wasser zu gelangen, um ihn zu durchschwimmen, mißlang.

An attempt to get to the open waters through the broad belt of reeds in order to swim across the river failed.

Ich geriet immer tiefer in den Morast hinein und wäre darin beinahe versunken.

I sunk ever deeper into the marsh and was nearly pulled under there.

Die schwarze Brühe reichte mir bis zur Brust, stinkende Blasen stiegen auf, und unter Aufbietung aller Kräfte zog ich mich am Schilfrohr wieder ans Ufer heran.

The black brew reached up to my chest, stinking bubbles rising up, and by gathering all my strength I pulled myself back to the shore again using the reeds.

Völlig verdreckt und erschöpft suchte ich eine freie Stelle im Schilfgürtel.

Completely dirty and exhausted, I was looking for an empty spot in the belt of reeds.

Dabei kam ich an eine Wochenendsiedlung, wie sie in Amerika sehr häufig zu finden sind.

In the process I came upon a settlement of weekend cottages, like are found frequently in America.

Es war gerade Samstag und überall standen Autos.

It was Saturday and there were cars everywhere.

Ich schlich mich an ein Häuschen heran.

I crept up to a little house.

Auf der Veranda saß ein junges Paar und unterhielt sich.

On the porch, a young couple sat and talked.

Dann kam ein zweites dazu, diese beiden hatten eine Bootsfahrt gemacht und trugen die Ruder mit sich.

Then a second couple joined them, these two had been boating and carried the oars with them.

Ich beobachtete, wie sie sie an die Hauswand lehnten und merkte mir die Stelle genau.

I observed how they leaned them against the house wall and memorized their precise location.

Dann wurde Licht in dem Häuschen gemacht; ich erblickte einige Würste und andere Eßvorräte im Vorraum und verspürte plötzlich einen gewaltigen Hunger.

Then a light came on in the little house; I spotted some sausages and other provisions in the front room and suddenly noticed my tremendous hunger.

Stunden vergingen.	Hours passed.
Endlich wurde das Licht gelöscht; man begab sich zur Ruhe.	Finally the light was turned off; everybody was getting their rest.
Auf Zehenspitzen schlich ich heran.	I snuck in on my tiptoes.
Gerade, als ich von der Veranda in den offenen Vorraum gelangen wollte, um eine Wurst zu ergreifen, hörte ich Flüstern.	Just as I was about to go from the porch into the front room to grab a sausage, I heard whispering.
Wie erstarrt blieb ich stehen …	I stopped as if paralyzed …
Dann vernahm ich zärtliche Worte – aha, die haben keine Zeit für andere; aber die Wurst konnte ich nicht holen, es war zu riskant.	Then I heard tender words – aha, they have no time for others; but I couldn't get the sausage, it was too risky.
Vorsichtig nahm ich die Ruder an mich und suchte am Fluß nach der Bootsanlegestelle.	Carefully I took the paddles and went to the river, looking for the dock.
Bald hatte ich sie gefunden.	Soon I had found it.
Gerade als ich eines der Boote losmachen wollte, blendete ein Autoscheinwerfer eines in der Nähe parkenden Kraftwagens auf; ich stand geblendet im vollen Licht.	Just as I was about to release the boat, the headlights of a nearby parked car lit up; I stood directly in the light, blinded.
Hatte man mich beobachtet?	Had I been observed?
Sollte ich jetzt noch ergriffen werden?	Would I now be caught again?
– Schnell hatte ich mich niedergeworfen und lauschte.	– I had quickly thrown myself down and listened.
Alles blieb ruhig – aber der Scheinwerfer leuchtete weiter; ich konnte mich nicht rühren.	Everything was quiet – but the headlights continued glowing; I couldn't budge.
Die Minuten schlichen dahin; wie lange lag ich nun schon am Boden?	The minutes crept by; how long had I been lying on the ground?

Fünf Minuten?

Eine halbe Stunde?

Ich weiß es nicht mehr.

Endlich erlosch das Licht.

Ich wartete noch eine Weile – aber es rührte sich nichts.

Vielleicht war es nur ein Liebespaar gewesen, das im Auto gesessen und mit dem Lichtschalter gespielt hatte?

Nur schnell jetzt, dachte ich, ehe das Licht wieder angeht.

Rasch hatte ich das Boot losgeknüpft, stieß ab und befand mich bald auf dem Strom.

Leise glitt der Nachen durchs Wasser, hin und wieder glucksten die Wellen, der Schrei eines Nachtvogels hallte an mein Ohr.

Sonst war alles still.

Silbern schimmerte der Strom im Mondlicht.

Die bezaubernde Romantik jener Augustnacht hätte ich sicher noch mehr genossen, wenn ich mich nicht in unmittelbarer Nähe der Grenze nach USA befunden hätte.

So aber mußte ich mich ganz auf ein etliche 100 Meter weiter südlich patroullierendes Polizeiboot konzentrieren, das plötzlich halb links vor mir aufgetaucht war.

Five minutes?

Half an hour?

I didn't know anymore.

Finally the light went out.

I waited for a while – but nothing was stirring.

Maybe it was just a couple in love, that were sitting in the car and had played with the light switch?

But hurry now, I thought, before the light goes back on.

Quickly I unhooked the boat, shoved off and soon found myself on the river.

Quietly the dinghy glided through the water, now and again the waves broke, the call of a night bird echoed in my ear.

Otherwise everything was silent.

The river shimmered silver in the moonlight.

I would certainly have enjoyed the magic romance of that August night even more, if I hadn't been in the immediate vicinity of the US border.

But I had to focus entirely on a police boat 100 meters to the south that had suddenly appeared on my left.

It searched the stream with its floodlight, but luckily didn't spot me.

I finally reached the opposite shore, threw the paddles in the reeds, pushed the boat back into the river to fake the accidental release of the boat, and had soon disappeared among the grasslands and pastures."

"How did you manage to find the camp at night?" Heinz threw out a question when I took a break from my tale to throw a few fresh pieces of wood onto the fire.

"It wasn't very hard, because the glare of the fence lighting was visible from far away.

I came to the camp from the south over a ridge that was covered in a sparse forest.

Through the last scattered trees, I could already see the sports field some 300 meters away in bright moonlight and I was just deliberating how I should sneak up on it

– then suddenly, as if they grew out of the earth, three guards stood in front of me – not ten steps separating us.

"Hands up!" I was told simultaneously from multiple sides.

VII

Wieder gefangen

Ich vernahm das Durchladen von Gewehren.

Der mir am nächsten stehende Posten brachte seinen Karabiner in Anschlag, ich blickte nach rechts – auch da stand bereits ein Soldat – und hinter mir hörte ich Schritte.

Aus!

Fliehen war Selbstmord!

Ich war umzingelt.

Unendlich mühsam brachte ich meine Arme in die Höhe; schon hatten mich kräftige Fäuste gepackt, schoben mich in Richtung des Lagers, führten mich ab.

Captured again

I heard the loading of rifles.

The guard closest to me leveled his rifle, I looked to the right – a soldier was already standing there – and I heard steps behind me.

Over!

Fleeing was suicide!

I was surrounded.

With endless effort I stuck my arms up; strong fists had already grabbed me, pushed me toward the camp, led me away.

überall wurde es lebendig; halb rechts erblickte ich drei weitere Posten, auf dem Weg zum Lager begegneten wir dem Sergeanten, der mich sogleich in Empfang nahm.

Everything was coming to life; halfway to the right I spotted three additional guards, on the way to the camp we met the sergeant, who received me at once.

Kaum im Wachlokal angekommen, erschien bereits der Kommandant mit seinem Adjutanten, gleich hinter ihm der kanadische Lagerdolmetscher.

Scarcely arrived in the guardroom, the commander already appeared with his adjutant, directly behind him the Canadian camp interpreter.

Sämtliche Offiziere waren auf den Beinen.

All officers were on their feet.

Und das alles in der Nacht zwischen 3 und 4 Uhr.

And all of this during the night between 3 and 4 a.m.

Ich war völlig überrascht; als wenn man mich erwartet hätte.

I was completely surprised; as if they had expected me.

Wie war das möglich?

How was that possible?

Ich kam gar nicht zum Nachdenken.

I mulled it over but had no idea.

Mit ausgesuchter Höflichkeit wurde ich in die Offiziersmesse gebeten, man bot mir zu essen und zu trinken.

With exquisite politeness, I was invited to go into the officer's mess where I was allowed to eat and to drink.

„Wünschen Sie den Whisky mit Soda oder pure?" fragte mich der Dolmetscher im Auftrag des Kommandanten.

"Would you like the whiskey straight up or with soda?" the interpreter asked me on behalf of the commander.

Ich langte herzhaft zu; es schmeckte mir großartig.

I helped myself heartily; it tasted magnificent.

„Und nun erzählen Sie uns mal, wie Sie das Bravourstückchen fertig gebracht haben", forderte mich der Dolmetscher auf, als ich den ersten Hunger gestillt hatte, „und die Adresse Ihres Helfers außerhalb des Lagers können Sie uns auch gleich nennen;

"And now do tell us how you pulled off this bit of boldness," challenged the interpreter after I had satisfied my initial hunger, "and you can also give us the address of your helpers outside the camp;

Sie brauchen nicht zu glauben, daß wir so dumm wären, und nichts von Ihren Vorbereitungen gemerkt hätten."

you shouldn't believe that we were so dumb, and noticed none of your preparations."

Ich stellte mich dumm und machte unklare Angaben; es sei mir eben zu langweilig im Lager gewesen.

I played dumb and made vague statements; it had just been too boring for me in the camp.

„Und wie kommen Sie dazu?" schrie mich der Dolmetscher an und knallte mir einen unserer wunderbar gefälschten Personalausweise auf den Tisch.

"And how did you get hold of this?" yelled the interpreter at me and slammed one of our wonderfully forged IDs onto the table.

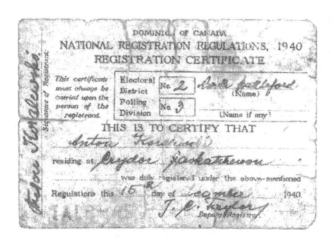

Dieser Ausweis mußte den Kanadiern allerdings einige Rätsel aufgeben, denn er war echt und zugleich gefälscht.

This ID must have given the Canadians quite a puzzle, because it was real and forged at the same time.

Die Schrift, das Papier, die Druckerschwärze waren echt – und doch war er im Lager gedruckt worden von deutschen Kriegsgefangenen.

The writing, the paper and the ink were real – but it had been printed in the camp by German POWs.

In mühevoller Arbeit hatte ein Amateur-Graphiker auf eine sorgsam polierte Grammophonplatte den gesamten kanadischen Personalausweis nach einer Zeitungsvorlage spiegelbildlich eingraviert.

With great efforts, an amateur graphic designer had engraved the complete mirrored Canadian ID from a template out of a newspaper onto a carefully polished gramophone disc.

Mit selbsthergestellter Druckerschwärze waren dann im Tiefdruckverfahren die benötigten Ausweise gedruckt worden.

With self-made printer's ink, the needed IDs had been gravure printed.

Die Ausklügelung dieses Verfahrens und die Herstellung der beiden ersten brauchbaren Druckplatten hatte weit über ein Jahr gedauert.

The perfection of the process and the production of the first usable printing discs had taken well over a year.

Die Kanadier standen vor einem Rätsel.

The Canadians were completely baffled.

Sie glaubten, uns wären diese Ausweise von außen ins Lager geschmuggelt worden.

They believed the IDs had been smuggled to us from outside the camp.

Daher die Frage nach unserem Helfer.

Hence the question about our helpers.

Sie brachten aber nichts aus mir heraus.

But they got nothing out of me.

Umgekehrt entnahm ich aus einigen zwischen dem Kommandanten und dem Dolmetscher gewechselten Worten, von denen sie glaubten, daß ich sie nicht verstünde:

Conversely, I learned quite a bit from the words exchanged between the commander and the interpreter, when they thought I couldn't understand them:

daß ihnen unser U-Bootplan bekannt war und daß weit im Umkreis vom Lager Posten aufgestellt waren, um jedes ausbrechenden Kriegsgefangenen auch sicher habhaft zu werden.

that our submarine plan was known to them and that guards had been posted in a perimeter around the camp to ensure that every escaping POW would be captured.

Solch einem Außenposten war ich beim Anschleichen an das Lager in die Arme gelaufen.

I had run right into the arms of those guards while sneaking in to the camp.

Ein ausgesuchtes Pech!

Quite a misfortune!

Jetzt wurde mir auch klar, warum die Kanadier nachts alle auf den Beinen waren; sie erwarteten allem Anschein nach noch andere Kriegsgefangene, die versuchen würden, zu entfliehen, um das U-Boot zu erreichen.

Now it was also clear to me why the Canadians were on their feet that night; by all appearances, they expected other POWs to try to break out in order to reach the submarine.

Auf einer Insel im St.-Lorenz-Strom interniert

Detained on an island in the St. Lawrence River

Im Morgengrauen wurde ich unter schwerer Bedeckung im Auto nach Montreal gebracht.

At daybreak, I was brought by car to Montreal under heavy guard.

Als die Sonne im Osten aufging, schlossen sich die schweren Eisentore eines alten Forts auf einer Insel im St. Lorenz-Strom hinter mir.

As the sun started rising in the east, the heavy iron gates of an old fort on an island in the St. Lawrence River were closing behind me.

Vier lange Wochen verbrachte ich in einer Kasematte dieses Forts.

Four long weeks I spent in a casemate in this fort.

Zwei Stunden pro Tag kam ich ans Tageslicht, wenn ich zu einem Spaziergang hinausgeholt wurde.

Two hours a day I got daylight, when I was taken outside for a walk.

Traurig blickte ich über das Wasser, sah den Schiffen nach, die stromauf und stromab fuhren, schaute hinüber auf die Weltstadt Montreal mit ihren Hochhäusern und Wolkenkratzern und ihrem Wahrzeichen, dem Mont Royal,

und folgte mit sehnsüchtigen Blicken den startenden Flugzeugen, die auf dem hinter der Stadt gelegenen Flugplatz Dorval ihren Flug über den Atlantik begannen.

Aber auch diese Zeit ging zu Ende, und eines Tages wurde ich in ein mir bis dahin nicht bekanntes Kriegsgefangenenlager im Staate Ontario gebracht, wo ich dich dann ja kennenlernte."

„Ja, ja", meinte Heinz, und stocherte nachdenklich in der Glut, „ein wenig Glück muß man schon beim Ausbrechen haben.

Hoffen wir, daß es uns treu bleibt, wenn wir nun morgen diesen uns so lieb gewordenen Platz hier verlassen."

Sadly I looked across the water, watched the ships that traveled upstream and downstream, gazed across at the cosmopolitan city of Montreal with its tall buildings and skyscrapers and its landmark, Mont Royal,

and my longing gaze followed the planes taking off from the Dorval airstrip located behind the city to begin their transatlantic flight.

But even that period came to an end, and one day I was taken to a prison camp in the province of Ontario that was unknown to me until that time, where I then got to know you."

"Yeah, yeah," said Heinz, and poked at the embers lost in thought, "one really must have a little luck to escape.

Let's hope that it sticks with us when we leave this beloved place tomorrow."

VIII

Über das Eis des Athabaska

Unsere Vorräte waren zu Ende; eine Ergänzung war nicht möglich, und wir mußten versuchen, das uns beschriebene Lager am Athabaska-River zu finden.

Am nächsten Tag vergruben wir alles, was wir nicht mitnehmen konnten, ebneten die Feuerstelle ein und brachen zu einem Gewaltmarsch auf.

Ungefähr 40 Meilen (64 km) lagen vor uns; wir wollten versuchen, sie auf einmal zu bewältigen.

In den Nachmittagsstunden, wir mochten gerade zwei Stunden unterwegs gewesen sein, verfinsterte sich der Himmel; ein fürchterlicher Blizzard brach herein.

Crossing the ice of the Athabasca

Our supplies were used up; restocking was not possible, and we must try to find the described camp on the Athabasca River.

The next day we buried everything we couldn't take with us, leveled the campfire and started out on a fast-paced march.

About 40 miles (64 kilometers) lay ahead of us; we wanted to try to conquer them in one go.

In the afternoon, we might have been underway about two hours, the sky darkened; a fearsome blizzard broke out.

Der Sturm heulte, die Bäume ächzten; wie mit Nadeln stachen die Schneeflocken ins Gesicht.

In einer Dickung fanden wir leidlichen Schutz.

Glücklicherweise hatte uns nur ein Ausläufer des Unwetters erreicht, und so konnten wir nach einiger Zeit unseren Marsch fortsetzen.

Aber ein neues Mißgeschick traf uns; ich verstauchte mir das Knie.

Mühsam erreichten wir den Alaska-Highway, eine während des Krieges erbaute Straße von Kanada nach Alaska.

Dort tat ich mich etwas leichter und bei Einbruch der Abenddämmerung erreichten wir den Strom Athabaska.

Obgleich es schon April war, bedeckte ihn noch eine dicke Eisdecke; sie sollte uns weiterhin als Weg dienen.

Besorgt streiften mich Heinzens Blicke.

Wirst du's auch schaffen mit deinem Knie, fragten seine Augen.

Keiner sprach ein Wort.

Etwa 30 Meilen lagen noch vor uns; 30 Meilen Eisstraße zwischen undurchdringlichem Urwald,

The storm howled, the trees groaned; the snow flakes stung like needles in the face.

In a thicket we found tolerable shelter.

Luckily we had only been caught in the edge of the storm, and so after a while we could resume our march.

But we were met with a new mishap; I twisted my knee.

With great difficulty we reached the Alaskan Highway, a road from Canada to Alaska built during the war.

Walking was easier for me there and as dawn broke we reached the Athabasca River.

Although it was already April, the stream was still covered with a thick ice blanket; that would serve as our path onward.

Heinz's worried glances fell on me.

Can you make it with your knee, his eyes were asking.

Nobody said a word.

About 30 miles still lay ahead of us; 30 miles of icy road between impenetrable forests,

30 Meilen Weg durch die Wildnis ohne eine menschliche Siedlung, ohne eine Möglichkeit der Hilfe, falls einer schlapp machen sollte,

30 Meilen nichts als Wald, Schnee und Eis.

Wir wagten es; wir mußten den Marsch wagen, wollten wir unsere Freiheit nicht aufgeben.

Rüstig schritten wir aus.

Das Eis war mit dünnem Firn bedeckt, der das Gehen sehr erleichterte; so kamen wir anfangs gut vorwärts.

Wir folgten einer alten Traktorenspur, die wohl von einem Holztransport herrühren mochte.

Sie erleichterte die Orientierung sehr, denn der Mond war noch nicht aufgegangen und es war ziemlich dunkel.

Plötzlich verlor sich die Spur im Nichts; wie angewurzelt blieben wir stehen – vor unseren Füßen gluckste und gurgelte das Wasser.

Ein eisiger Schreck durchfuhr uns, wären wir auch nur einen Schritt weitergegangen – riesengroß stand die Gefahr vor uns, in der wir wenige Augenblicke zuvor geschwebt hatten.

Heinz kniff mich in den Arm.

„Nochmal Schwein gehabt", meinte er kurz; seine Stimme klang heiser.

30 miles of path through the wilderness without any human settlement, without any possibility of help if we couldn't go any farther,

30 miles of nothing but woods, snow and ice.

We risked it; we must try the march if we didn't want to give up our freedom.

We strode off briskly.

The ice was covered with a thin layer of old snow, which made walking a lot easier; so at first we made good progress.

We followed an old tractor path, which was probably made by a timber transport.

It greatly simplified navigation, since the moon had not yet risen and it was rather dark.

Suddenly the path faded into nothing; we stopped dead in our tracks – the water chortled and gurgled right in front of our feet.

A freezing shock ran through us, if we had only taken one more step – the enormous danger stood there, we had almost gone in only a few moments before.

Heinz pinched me in the arm.

"Lucky again," he said shortly; his voice sounded hoarse.

„Die Tage sind eben doch schon verdammt warm; in ein paar Wochen ist das Eis aufgebrochen.

– Höchste Zeit, daß der Mond aufgeht", erwiderte ich.

Um Mitternacht stand der Mond so hoch, daß wir einen Eindruck von der Wildheit der Landschaft erhielten.

Überall am Ufer lagen hoch übereinander-getürmt entwurzelte Baumriesen, vom Hochwasser herangeschwemmt.

Urgewaltig mußte das Wasser im Frühjahr daherbrausen.

Gespenstisch ragten die kahlen Wurzeln in die Luft.

Einsam und schweigend stand der Urwald wie eine stumme Mauer dahinter.

Der Weg wurde immer beschwerlicher; hoch aufgetürmt stellten sich uns Eisschollen in den Weg, ein großes Packeisfeld dehnte sich vor uns.

Mühsam bahnten wir uns einen Weg hindurch; immer wieder brachen wir durch die obersten dünnen Eisschichten, fanden glücklicherweise etwas tiefer wieder Halt, waren aber bald weit über die Knie durchnäßt.

Am Ufer zwischen Wurzelwerk und Gestrüpp war der Weg nicht besser.

Als wir nach Stunden das Packeisfeld hinter uns hatten, streikte mein verrenktes Knie.

"The days are already damn warm; in a few weeks the ice will be broken.

– High time for the moon to rise," I replied.

Around midnight, the moon was high enough that we got a good look at the savagery of the landscape.

Everywhere along the riverbank, piles of uprooted trees lay intertwined, placed there by floods.

The water must roar through here during springtime.

Eerily the bare roots rose into the air.

Lonely and silent, the wilderness stood behind as a mute wall.

The path became increasingly difficult; tall stacked ice floes were blocking the way, a huge field of pack ice spread out before us.

Arduously we made a way through; repeatedly we broke through the topmost layers of thin ice, luckily always finding a foothold somewhat deeper, but soon were soaked far above the knees.

On the shore, between roots and undergrowth, the path was no better.

When we left the field of pack ice behind us after several hours, my twisted knee gave out.

Heinz bettete mich in den Schnee, versuchte mit klammen Fingern mein Knie zu massieren.

Weitab jede Hilfe.

Unsere Situation war verzweifelt.

Wie lange ich gelegen hatte, weiß ich nicht mehr genau; auf einmal hielt Heinz mit der Massage inne und deutete auf das gegenüberliegende Ufer: zwei dunkle Kolosse trabten dort entlang – Bären!

Plötzlich verhofften sie – anscheinend hatten sie Wind von uns bekommen.

Deutlich konnten wir sie im hellen Mondlicht erkennen.

Was würden sie tun?

Nach einer Weile setzten sie jedoch ihren Weg fort, ohne sich weiter um uns zu kümmern und waren bald im Ufergehölz verschwunden.

„Versuchen wir es noch mal!" sagte ich nach einer Weile, „liegenbleiben kann ich hier schließlich nicht – und einmal müssen wir ja nach Chisholm kommen, das Lager soll doch direkt am Strom liegen."

„Stütze dich nur kräftig auf mich!" forderte mich Heinz auf, obgleich er kleiner und schmächtiger war als ich und selbst der Erschöpfung nahe, „bald haben wir es geschafft."

Heinz lay me down in the snow, tried to massage my knee with his damp fingers.

Any help was far away.

Our situation was desperate.

How long I had been lying there, I no longer remember; all of a sudden Heinz stopped the massage and pointed toward the opposite shore: there, two dark hulks were trotting along – bears!

Suddenly they became alert – apparently they must have gotten wind of us.

We could see them clearly in the bright moonlight.

What would they do?

After a while they continued on their journey, without worrying about us any longer and soon they had disappeared into the woods along the shore.

"Let's try it again!" I said after a while, "I can't just keep lying here – and at some point we have to reach Chisholm, the camp should lie directly on the river."

"Just lean heavily on me!" offered Heinz, even though he was smaller and lankier than I and near exhaustion himself, "we'll have made it soon."

– Niemals habe ich seine Kameradschaft stärker empfunden, als in jenen Stunden.

Das Ausruhen und Massieren hatte tatsächlich etwas geholfen, und wir kamen leidlich vorwärts.

Wie weit wir allerdings noch von unserem Ziel entfernt waren, wußten wir nicht, denn wir hatten jegliches Gefühl für die zurückgelegte Entfernung verloren.

Dazu kam, daß der Strom große Kurven beschrieb, die wir sämtlich auslaufen mußten, da ein Abschneiden wegen des dichten Ufergestrüpps ausgeschlossen war.

Glücklicherweise besserte sich der Zustand des Eises etwas, die Oberfläche wurde glatt, so daß wir die Füße nicht mehr zu heben brauchten, was meinem Knie sehr gut tat.

So torkelten wir mehr als wir gingen Stunde um Stunde dahin.

Immer häufiger mußten wir Ruhepausen einlegen, immer öfter versagte mein defektes Knie.

Während wir anfangs meist einen Baumstamm am Ufer zum Rasten benutzten, legten wir uns gegen Morgen einfach dort hin, wo wir gerade standen, und es kostete uns alle Willenskraft, nicht einzuschlafen.

In jener Nacht habe ich erlebt, was die Einbildungskraft vermag;

– Never have I felt his companionship more strongly than during those hours.

The resting and massaging had actually helped somewhat, and we made tolerable progress.

How far we actually still were from our destination, we didn't know because we had lost track of the distance we had covered.

In addition to that, the stream made large curves, which we had to follow since cutting across was impossible due to the thick undergrowth on the shore.

Luckily the ice's condition was improving somewhat, the surface became smooth, so that we didn't need to lift our feet any more, which did my knee some good.

So we stumbled more than walked, hour after hour onward.

Ever more frequently we had to take a break, ever more often my bad knee gave out.

While at the beginning we had mostly used a log on the shore for resting, toward morning we would simply lay down, wherever we happened to be standing, and it took all our willpower not to fall asleep.

On that night I witnessed the power of imagination;

obgleich es völlig ausgeschlossen war, vor einer gewissen zurückgelegten Entfernung Häuser und Straßen anzutreffen, war der Wunsch, eine menschliche Behausung zu finden, so groß in uns, daß wir hinter jedem Schatten eine Hütte zu sehen glaubten;

einmal meinten wir auch am gegenüberliegenden Ufer eine Rampe mit Zufahrtstraße zu erblicken.

Wir waren so überzeugt davon, daß wir trotz unserer Erschöpfung hinübergingen – als wir aber dort anlangten, fanden wir nichts als Schnee und einige umgestürzte Bäume.

Gegen 6 Uhr morgens begann es zu dämmern.

Wir fanden eine günstige offene Stelle im Eis, legten uns flach hin und tranken das klare, frische Wasser; wir benetzten auch das Gesicht, um etwas munter zu werden.

Langsam rötete sich der Himmel im Osten; wenn wir nicht bald das Lager erreichten, war es unmöglich, ungesehen hineinzuschlüpfen.

Verzweifelt suchten wir die Ufer ab.

Wir waren nun 18 Stunden ununterbrochen unterwegs und hatten trotz unseres langsamen Tempos doch eine schöne Strecke zurückgelegt; weit konnten wir nicht mehr vom Ziel entfernt sein.

even though it was completely impossible to find houses and roads after having travelled such distance, the desire to find some human dwelling was so great inside us, that behind every shadow we believed we saw a cabin;

once, we thought we saw a ramp with an access road on the opposite shore.

We were so convinced of it, that we went over despite our fatigue – but when we arrived, we found nothing but snow and some fallen trees.

About 6 o'clock in the morning it began to get light.

We found a good open spot in the ice, lay down flat and drank the clear, fresh water; we also splashed our faces to become somewhat more alert.

Slowly the eastern sky turned red; if we didn't reach the camp soon it would be impossible to slip in unseen.

Desperately we scanned the shores.

We had now been walking continuously for 18 hours and despite our slow speed we had put quite some distance behind us; we couldn't be far away from our destination.

IX

Im Lager Chisholm

Plötzlich kniff mich Heinz in den Arm;
mit der Rechten deutete er zum Ufer:
„Diesmal ist es keine Einbildung, dort
drüben sind Häuser!" stieß er hervor.

Auch ich erkannte sie; ohne Zweifel –
Giebel richtiger Häuser hoben sich
gegen den östlichen Himmel ab – wir
waren am Ziel!

Die Erschöpfung war verschwunden,
neue Kräfte belebten uns.

Rasch hatten wir das Ufer erreicht,
erklommen die Böschung und
gelangten auf einen großen Fabrikhof.

Dort trennten wir uns, um nicht beide,
sollten wir Pech haben,
wiederergriffen zu werden.

In Camp Chisholm

Heinz suddenly poked me in the
arm; with his right hand he pointed
to the shore: "This time it's no
illusion, there are houses over
there!" he exclaimed.

I recognized them too, without a
doubt – the gables of actual houses
were rising toward the eastern sky –
we had reached our destination!

The fatigue had disappeared, new
powers enlivened us.

Quickly we reached the shore,
climbed the embankment and came
to a huge factory yard.

There we split up so both of us
wouldn't be captured if misfortune
should strike.

Während sich Heinz verborgen hielt, ging ich auf die Suche nach den von deutschen Kriegsgefangenen bewohnten Blockhütten.

Sollte ich dabei erwischt werden, würde er als der Gesunde die größere Chance zum Durchkommen haben.

Auf dem Fabrikhof herrschte noch völlige Stille – die Arbeit in der Sägemühle ruhte – es war Karfreitag.

Die Gedanken flogen zurück; in der Nacht zum Karfreitag war ich vor vier Jahren in Gefangenschaft geraten; damals hatte ich die Freiheit verloren – nun besaß ich sie wieder, wollte sie nicht mehr preisgeben!

Vorsichtig schlich ich um die Hütten herum; nur jetzt nicht die falsche erwischen.

Endlich faßte ich mir ein Herz, trat vorsichtig in eine hinein und zog die Tür hinter mir zu.

Eine Weile verharrte ich regungslos.

Zunächst vernahm ich nur das Schnarchen schlafender Männer.

Als sich meine Augen an das Halbdunkel im Innern gewöhnt hatten, konnte ich eine Reihe Bettstellen mit schlafenden Gestalten erkennen.

Waren es kanadische Zivilarbeiter oder deutsche Kriegsgefangene?

Bis aufs äußerste gespannt waren die Nerven.

While Heinz stayed hidden, I went on the search for the log huts inhabited by the German POWs.

Should I have been caught doing this, he as the healthy one would have a greater chance of pulling through.

Complete silence prevailed at the factory yard – work in the sawmill was at a rest – it was Good Friday.

My thoughts flew back; on the eve of Good Friday four years ago I had been captured; that's when I had lost my freedom – now I possessed it again, did not want to relinquish it!

Carefully I crept around the huts; just don't get the wrong one.

Finally I mustered the courage, stepped cautiously inside one and pulled the door shut behind me.

For awhile I remained motionless.

At first, I only heard the snore of sleeping men.

After my eyes had adjusted to the semidarkness inside, I could recognize a row of beds with sleeping figures.

Were they Canadian workers or German POWs?

My nerves were stretched to the limit.

Behutsam untersuchte ich einige Kleidungsstücke – nichts deutete darauf hin, daß sie Deutschen gehörten.

Langsam tastete ich mich durch den ganzen Raum … wollte das gegenüberliegende Fenster erreichen – da – sprach dort nicht jemand?

– unvermittelt blieb ich stehen, gebannt starrte ich nach links – heiß und kalt lief es mir über den Rücken.

Dann verloren sich die Worte in undeutliches Gemurmel, jemand hatte geträumt; war es englisch oder deutsch gewesen?

Ich war mir nicht darüber im klaren.

Cautiously I examined a few articles of clothing – nothing about them suggested they belonged to Germans.

Slowly I fumbled across the entire room … wanted to reach the opposite window – there – didn't someone speak over there?

– abruptly I stopped; mesmerized I peered to the left – hot and cold chills ran up my back.

Then the words lost themselves in garbled muttering, somebody had been dreaming; was it English or German?

I was not sure about that.

Eine Mütze mit deutscher Kokarde

A hat with a German cockade

Am Fenstergriff hing eine Mütze; ich nahm sie herunter, hielt sie dicht vor die Augen, schaute – schaute …

– ja, tatsächlich, eine deutsche Kokarde war vorn zu erkennen – eine Mütze des deutschen Afrikakorps!

Schnell weckte ich den mir zunächst liegenden Schläfer, der mir – oh welche Wonne! – sogleich in echtem Schwäbisch Bescheid gab; er war von Aalen!

A hat was hanging on the window handle; I took it down, held it close to my eyes, looked – looked …

– yes, indeed, a German cockade was discernible on the front – a hat from the German Africa Corps!

Quickly I woke the sleeping guy lying closest to me, who – oh how delightful! – immediately gave me a reply in true Swabian dialect; he was from Aalen!

Nun löste sich die Spannung; wir schüttelten uns die Hände und ich gab ihm rasch die nötigen Erklärungen.

The tension disappeared; we shook hands and I quickly explained everything necessary.

Auf einmal war die ganze Hütte auf den Beinen, Heinz wurde herangeholt, und dann saßen wir eine Viertelstunde später alle gemütlich um einen Tisch.

At once, the whole hut came to life, Heinz was brought in, and a quarter of an hour later we were all sitting comfortably around a table.

Im Ofen knisterte das Feuer, auf dem Tisch dampfte der Kaffee, und zwölf brave deutsche Kriegsgefangene lauschten gespannt unserer Erzählung.

The fire crackled in the stove, coffee was steaming on the table, and twelve good German POWs listened intently to our story.

Wir waren gerade mitten im Erzählen, da erscholl der Ruf:

We were right in the middle of the tale, when the call rang out:

„Die Mounted Police ist im Lager!"

"The Mounted Police are in the camp!"

Ein heftiger Schreck durchfuhr uns.

A severe shock ran through us.

In Windeseile war Heinz in einem selbstgezimmerten Schrankkoffer und ich auf dem Boden verschwunden.

As fast as the wind, Heinz had disappeared into a homemade trunk and I below the floor.

Der deutsche Lagerführer begab sich hinaus …

The German camp leader walked outside …

und konnte aus dem Gespräch zwischen dem Constabler und dem wachhabenden Korporal entnehmen, daß sich in den Wäldern 40 Meilen weiter nördlich zwei deutsche Kriegsgefangene herumtrieben, die versuchen könnten, sich in dieses Lager einzuschleichen;

and was able to tell from the conversation between the Constable and the corporal on duty that two POWs were running around in the woods 40 miles north of here and they might try to sneak into this camp;

der Korporal solle entsprechende Vorsichtsmaßnahmen treffen.

the corporal should take appropriate precautionary measures.

Erleichtert vernahmen wir diese Nachricht, man vermutete uns also nicht in Chisholm.

We were relieved to hear this news, they did not suspect we were in Chisholm.

70

Vorbereitungen zur Fahrt in die USA

Zehn Tage blieben wir in diesem Lager.

Die Bewachung war nicht sehr streng;

die Wachposten kamen selten in die Hütten, und wenn einer erschien, waren wir durch einen gut organisierten Warndienst rechtzeitig unterrichtet – und verschwanden durch eine unauffällige Falltür unter dem Fußboden.

Dieses Versteck hatten wir uns gleich am ersten Tag, nachdem wir gründlich ausgeschlafen hatten, gebaut, um auch bei einer Durchsuchung nicht gefunden zu werden.

Während dieser Zeit vervollständigten wir unsere Fluchtausrüstung.

In selbstloser Weise wurden wir dabei von unseren Kameraden unterstützt.

Aus einer Decke entstand eine Zivilhose, ein alter Hut wurde aufgemöbelt, eine neue Mütze geschneidert.

Daneben zeichneten wir Karten aus einem kanadischen Schulatlas ab, erneuerten unsere Ausweise mit selbstverfertigten Stempeln ...

und verdienten uns einige Cents durch Uhrenreparaturen, die ich durch Vermittlung eines Kameraden für einen Trapper ausführte.

Preparations for a journey to the USA

Ten days we stayed in this camp.

The security was not very strict;

the guards rarely came into the huts, and if one appeared, we were informed ahead of time through a well organized alert system – and disappeared below the floor through an unobtrusive trap door under the floor.

We had built this hideout the first day, after we had plenty of rest, to avoid being found in a thorough search.

During this time, we completed our escape gear.

In a selfless way, our comrades supported us here.

A blanket was turned into a pair of pants, an old hat was refurbished, a new cap sewn.

In addition, we copied maps out of a Canadian school atlas, restored our IDs with self-made stamps ...

and earned a few cents repairing watches, work that I did for a trapper with a comrade as go between.

Auch unser Äußeres veränderten wir; mit Hilfe von Wasserstoffsuperoxyd wurden meine dunklen Haare rotblond; ein Mittelscheitel und ein Schnurrbart taten das Übrige.

Schwieriger war das Dunkelfärben von Heinz' blonden Haaren.

Mehrere Versuche mit Schuhcreme scheiterten, und schließlich mußte er es aufgeben.

Nebenher hatten wir Gelegenheit zu Schach und anderen Spielen, konnten lesen und auch Musik hören, denn der YMCA (CVJM) hatte auch die entlegensten Holzfällerlager mit Büchern, Grammophonen und Schallplatten versorgt.

Ein wirklich leuchtendes Beispiel christlicher Nächstenliebe, wie es im Zweiten Weltkrieg wohl nicht häufig zu finden war.

Eines Abends kam einer unserer Kameraden von der Arbeit auf der Sägemühle zurück mit den Worten:

„Morgen wird ein Waggon für Rhode Island beladen; das wäre doch etwas für euch, da er zur Ostküste fährt."

Auf diesen Zufall hatten wir schon lange gehofft.

Ein Wagen, der durch den ganzen nordamerikanischen Kontinent ging – was wollten wir mehr?

We also changed our appearances; my dark hair was turned reddish blond using hydrogen peroxide; a center part and a mustache completed the look.

Dyeing Heinz's blond hair dark proved to be more difficult.

Several tries with shoe polish failed, and finally he had to give it up.

At the same time, we had the opportunity to play chess and other games, could read and also listen to music since the YMCA had supplied even the most remote lumberjack camps with books, gramophones and records.

A truly glowing example of christian charity, as was probably not common to find in the Second World War.

One evening one of our comrades returned from work in the sawmill with the words:

"Tomorrow a railway car set for Rhode Island will be loaded; that would be something for you, since it's headed to the East Coast."

Just the happenstance we had long been hoping for.

A train that went across the entire North American continent – what more would we want?

In dieser Nacht haben wir beide kaum ein Auge zugetan.

Sollte es wirklich klappen?

Alles wurde noch einmal überlegt, von neuem erwogen; nur jetzt nichts verkehrt machen.

Wenn der Absprung von hier unbemerkt gelang, dann hatten wir einen riesigen Schritt vorwärts getan.

Am letzten Tage drohte noch alles schief zu gehen.

Am Morgen veröffentlichte die „Edmonton Post" unseren Steckbrief mit dem Hinweis, daß wir uns möglicherweise in der Gegend von Chisholm aufhalten;

mittags brachte einer unserer Kameraden die Nachricht, daß unter den kanadischen Zivilarbeitern davon gesprochen würde, die zwei gesuchten deutschen Kriegsgefangenen würden im Lager Chisholm verborgen gehalten,

und kurz darauf kündigte der kanadische Korporal dem deutschen Lagerführer eine außerplanmäßige Zählung an.

„Nur nicht die Nerven verlieren", meinte Heinz, „so leicht lassen wir uns nicht erwischen."

That night, we both hardly slept a wink.

Would it really work?

Everything was pondered once more, considered anew; now was no time to screw up.

If our exit from here went unnoticed, then we would have made a huge step forward.

But on the last day, everything threatened to go wrong.

In the morning, the "Edmonton Post" published our wanted poster with the suggestion that we were possibly staying in the area around Chisholm;

at noon, one of our comrades brought the news that among the Canadian workers, it was being said that the two German POWs being sought were kept hidden in Camp Chisholm,

and shortly thereafter, the Canadian corporal informed the German camp commander of an unplanned count.

"Just don't lose your nerve," said Heinz, "we won't let ourselves be caught so easily."

„Also hinein in unser Versteck",
drängte ich; wenige Augenblicke
später schlossen sich die Dielen über
uns, ein Riegel wurde von unten davor
gelegt, der ein Abheben des Deckels
unmöglich machte …

und so warteten wir getrost der Dinge,
die da kommen sollten.

Zunächst blieb alles ruhig; träge
schlichen die Minuten dahin – wie
langsam doch die Zeit vergeht, wenn
man die Sekunden zählt.

Wir verfielen schließlich in einen
Dämmerzustand, aus dem wir
plötzlich durch herannahende Schritte
geweckt wurden, wir hielten den Atem
an; undeutliches Stimmengewirr drang
zu uns, suchte man uns bereits?

– dann entfernten sich die Schritte
wieder.

„Die Luft ist rein; ihr könnt wieder
raus!" vernahmen wir nach einer
Weile eine bekannte Stimme.

„Gott sei Dank", sagte ich und schob
den Riegel zurück.

Als wir den Deckel hochhoben,
brannte in der Baracke bereits Licht;
draußen war es schon dunkel!

„Schnell jetzt! Es wird Zeit, sonst
kommt ihr nicht mehr in den Waggon!"

Rasch waren wir draußen;

"OK, into our hideout," I urged; a
few moments later the floorboards
were put back into place above us, a
crossbar was secured from below to
make it impossible to lift our
covering …

and so we waited confidently for
anything that should come.

At first, everything remained quiet;
the minutes crept by sluggishly –
how slowly the time passes, when
you're counting the seconds.

We finally fell into a state of
semi-consciousness, out of which
we were suddenly woken by
approaching foot steps, we held our
breath; the sound of garbled voices
reached our ears, were they already
looking for us?

– then the steps departed again.

"The coast is clear; you can come
out again!" we heard a familiar
voice say after a while.

"Thank God," I said and removed
the crossbar.

After lifting up the lid, the lights
were already lit in the barrack again;
outside it was already dark!

"Hurry now! It's time, else you
won't make it into the railway car!"

Quickly we were outside;

alles war aufs beste vorbereitet: Proviant für fünf Tage, eine Wolldecke, ein Stück von einer Bandsäge, ein großer Schraubenbolzen als Hammer verwendbar, eine Dreikantfeile zum Nachschärfen der Säge, ein paar Nägel und ein Stemmeisen, Streichhölzer und eine Kerze.

So ausgerüstet wurden wir im Geleitzug zum Bahnkörper geführt.

In der Dunkelheit konnten wir kaum etwas erkennen; ein paar vereinzelte Lampen brannten im Fabrikhof.

Von rechts kam eine Gestalt auf uns zu.

Wir drückten uns an die Wand.

„Gut Freund", klang es gedämpft zu uns herüber.

„Soeben hat der Nachtwächter auf seiner Runde die Gleisanlagen passiert; in einer halben Stunde ist er frühestens wieder dort."

Wir schlichen weiter, von Spähern auf beiden Seiten gesichert.

Unbemerkt erreichten wir den Bahnkörper.

Dort stand unser Waggon.

everything was prepared perfectly: provisions for five days, a wool blanket, part of a band saw, a huge screw bolt usable as a hammer, a triangular file to re-sharpen the saw, a few nails and a crowbar, matches and a candle.

So equipped, we were escorted in a convoy to the rail bed.

We could barely discern anything in the darkness; a few lamps burned in the factory yard.

A figure was approaching from the right.

We pressed ourselves against the wall.

"Good friend" we heard a muted voice say.

"The night watchman just passed the railway tracks on his rounds; he won't be back for half an hour at the earliest."

We crept on, guarded by scouts on either side.

We reached the rail bed unnoticed.

There stood our railway car.

Mit ein paar Sätzen waren wir da, hilfreiche Arme halfen uns hinein, ein letzter Händedruck, ein letzter Gruß und Dank, und schon wurde die schwere Tür zugeschoben, der Riegel vorgelegt, hastig sich entfernende Schritte – wir waren allein.

Vorsichtig tasteten wir uns in der Dunkelheit nach oben; bis fast an die Decke war der Waggon mit Brettern beladen; ein schmaler Raum blieb frei, gerade groß genug, um einem erwachsenen Menschen in horizontaler Lage Platz zu gewähren.

Wir breiteten die Decke aus, legten uns nieder und lauschten.

Nach einer Weile vernahmen wir Schritte; langsam näherten sie sich, schlurften vorbei und verloren sich in der Ferne.

Der Nachtwächter hatte seine Runde gemacht – nichts hatte er bemerkt.

After a few movements we were there, helpful arms helped us inside, a last handshake, a last greeting and thanks, and already the heavy door was being pushed closed, the crossbar put in place, hasty steps were departing – we were alone.

Carefully we felt our way forward in the darkness; the car was loaded with boards almost up to the ceiling; a narrow space remained unused, just big enough to allow an adult to lay in a horizontal position.

We unfolded the blanket, lay down and listened.

After a while we heard steps; slowly they came nearer, shuffled by and then were lost in the distance.

The night watchman was making his rounds – he had noticed nothing.

X

Am Beginn einer neuen Etappe

Ein großes Glücksgefühl durchrieselte uns; wieder waren wir im letzten Augenblick einer gefährlichen Situation entronnen und standen am Beginn einer neuen Etappe unserer Flucht, von der wir nicht wußten, was sie uns bringen würde, von der wir uns aber vieles erhofften.

An Schlafen war auch in dieser Nacht nicht zu denken; viel zu aufgeregt waren wir, und dann machte sich die Kälte bald sehr bemerkbar, zumal wir uns wegen der enstehenden Geräusche nicht bewegen durften.

Gegen 6 Uhr früh hörten wir die Fabriksirene zur Arbeit rufen; bald vernahmen wir auch Leben auf dem Bahnkörper.

At the beginning of a new stage

An immense feeling of joy gushed through us; again we had escaped at the last minute from a dangerous situation and stood at the beginning of a new stage in our escape, we did not know what it would bring us, but we had many hopes.

We didn't even think about sleeping that night; we were much too excited, and then the cold soon made itself very apparent, especially since we were not allowed to move because of the resulting noises.

About 6 o'clock a.m. we heard the factory siren calling everyone to work; soon we noticed life on the rail bed.

Unser Waggon wurde plombiert, rangiert und mit anderen zu einem Zug zusammengestellt.

Our car was sealed, moved and assembled with other cars onto the train.

Schließlich fuhren wir ab.

Finally we departed.

„Ein Glück, daß es endlich losgeht, ich bin schon ganz steif; jetzt kann man sich wenigstens bewegen, ohne gleich gehört zu werden."

"What luck, that it's finally leaving, I am already quite stiff; now we can at least move around, without immediately being heard."

Ein ganz spärlicher Lichtschimmer drang durch einige Ritzen in unser Verließ, schwache Dämmerung verbreitend.

A quite meager glow of light pressed through a few cracks into our dungeon, faint dawn spreading.

Wir blickten uns um.

We looked around us.

Überall Bretter, nichts als Bretter.

Boards everywhere, nothing but boards.

In der Mitte des Waggons war ein Raum ausgespart, der zum Einsteigen und Beladen gedient hatte.

In the middle of the car was a space left open, it had served for entering and loading.

Dort konnten wir wenigstens stehen.

There we could at least stand up.

Die Eisenbahngüterwaggons sind in Nordamerika bedeutend größer und stabiler als bei uns in Europa; wegen der langen Zeit, die die Wagen auf der Strecke liegen, sind sie fast alle geschlossen.

The freight cars in North America are considerably larger and more stable than they are in Europe; because of the amount of time they spend sitting on the tracks, almost all are closed off.

Dicke Eichenbohlen an Wänden und Boden und ein Dach aus Stahlblech.

Thick oak boards on the walls and floor, and a roof made of steel panels.

Puffer sind keine vorhanden, und die Verbindung zwischen zwei Waggons wird durch eine besondere Kuppelung hergestellt, die durch kräftiges Zusammenstoßen zum Einschnappen gebracht wird.

Buffers were not in place, and the connection between two cars was made through a special coupling, brought into a snapped position by pushing forcefully together.

Gleich zu Anfang der Fahrt begannen wir eine Art Log-Buch zu führen, das heißt wir verzeichneten auf einem Bogen Papier, den wir eigens für diesen Zweck vorbereitet hatten, die Fahrzeit, die Fahrtrichtung und die geschätzte Fahrgeschwindigkeit;

Right at the start of our trip we began to keep a sort of log book, on a sheet of paper specifically prepared for this purpose, meaning we listed the driving time, driving direction and estimated speed;

auf diese Weise trieben wir eine grobe Koppelnavigation, die uns ermöglichte, uns einen ungefähren Begriff über unseren jeweiligen Standort zu machen.

that way we had a rough 'dead reckoning' that made it possible for us to have an approximate notion of our location at any given time.

Um nicht ganz von der Außenwelt abgeschnitten zu sein, stemmten wir noch ein kleines Guckloch in die Wand.

In order to not be fully cut off from the outside world, we made a small peephole in the wall.

Durch dieses hindurch sahen wir die Landschaft an uns vorüberziehen und konnten hin und wieder sogar den Namen einer Station erkennen.

Through this hole we watched the landscape passing by and could every now and then discern the name of a station.

Die wichtigste Arbeit aber war die Herstellung eines Ausstiegloches.

The most important work however was the creation of an exit hole.

Damit begannen wir gleich nach der Abfahrt.

That we began right after the departure.

Neben der Tür war ein schmaler Raum frei geblieben, so daß wir unmittelbaren Zugang zum Boden hatten.

Next to the door a narrow space was left open, so that we had direct access to the floor.

Hier entstand allmählich eine Öffnung, groß genug, um uns durchschlüpfen zu lassen.

Here we gradually created an opening, big enough to allow us to slip through.

Am Abend des ersten Tages waren wir bereits in Edmonton.

By the evening of the first day we were already in Edmonton.

In der Nacht wurden wir zu einem neuen Zug zusammengestellt und in östlicher Richtung auf Fahrt geschickt.

Die Gegend, durch die wir in den Vormittagsstunden fuhren, kam uns merkwürdig bekannt vor, und unser Erstaunen und die Freude waren groß, als wir um Mittag in Wainwright hielten.

Hier hatten wir unseren Weg vor drei Wochen begonnen, hier lag ja unser Gefangenenlager, dessen Wachtürme wir deutlich erkennen konnten, hier wußten wir viele Kameraden, deren heiße Wünsche uns begleiteten.

Plötzlich fühlten wir uns dem Kriegsgefangenendasein wieder ganz nahe, dem wir durch die Erlebnisse der letzten Wochen schon weit entrückt waren.

„Weißt du noch, wie oft wir dort oben hinter dem Zaun standen und mit sehnsüchtigen Blicken den Zügen nachschauten?" flüsterte ich versonnen.

„Und welche Umwege mußten wir machen, um in diesen Waggon zu gelangen!" erwiderte Heinz; und nach einer Weile: „Der Erfolg will erkämpft sein; die schönsten Früchte fallen uns nicht mühelos in den Schoß …"

During the night we were re-assembled onto a new train and sent eastward.

The scenery we passed through during the morning hours looked strangely familiar, and our astonishment and joy were immense when we stopped around mid day in Wainwright.

Here we had begun our journey three weeks ago, here lay our prison camp, whose watchtowers we could clearly discern, here we knew many comrades, whose good wishes accompanied us.

Suddenly we felt the POW life was again quite near, something that was already far removed through the experiences of the past weeks.

"Do you still remember how often we stood up there behind that fence and gazed with longing stares at the trains?" I whispered.

"And what detours we had to take, in order to get into this car!" replied Heinz; and after a while: "Success wants to be fought for; the best fruits don't fall effortlessly into one's lap …"

Halt in Winnipeg

Nach kurzem Aufenthalt ging die Fahrt weiter; wir fuhren mit einigen Unterbrechungen den ganzen Tag, die darauffolgende Nacht und den nächsten Tag durch.

Dann trafen wir in Winnipeg ein.

Diese Stadt nimmt für sich den Ruf in Anspruch, zu den kältesten Städten der Erde zu gehören; wir haben das während unseres 24stündigen Aufenthaltes dort gründlich zu spüren bekommen.

Aber nicht so sehr die Kälte war es, die uns zu schaffen machte, größeren Kummer bereiteten uns die schwindenden Eßvorräte.

Wir waren jetzt drei Tage unterwegs und hatten bereits beginnen müssen, die Verpflegung zu rationieren.

Dazu trat eine weitere Sorge: in Winnipeg wurden wir viel hin- und herrangiert; dabei ging man nicht gerade vorsichtig mit uns um, der Wagen enthielt ja schließlich „nur Holz" und konnte schon ein paar Stöße vertragen.

Da es sich aber um gehobelte Bretter handelte, gerieten diese durch die Erschütterung ins Rutschen und schoben sich langsam über unser gerade fertiggestelltes Ausstiegloch.

Stopover in Winnipeg

After a short break the journey continued; we traveled the entire day, the following night and the next day with only minor interruptions.

Then we reached Winnipeg.

This city makes a claim to be among the coldest cities on Earth; we thoroughly experienced that during our 24-hour stopover.

But it wasn't really the cold that occupied us, of bigger concern to us was the dwindling food supply.

We had now been underway for three days and already had to begin to ration the food.

Another worry was added: in Winnipeg we were moved back and forth a lot; in the process they weren't very careful with us, the freight car contained, after all, "just wood" and could certainly handle a few bumps.

But since the wood consisted of planed boards, they were set in motion by the jarring and slowly slid over our recently completed exit hole.

Wir machten verzweifelte Anstrengungen, durch Abstützungen die Holzmassen am Weiterrutschen zu hindern, doch hatten wir damit nur vorübergehend Erfolg; über kurz oder lang brachen unsere mit unzureichenden Mitteln erstellten Konstruktionen immer wieder zusammen.

We undertook desperate efforts, supporting the mass of wood to hinder it from moving farther, but there we had only temporary success; sooner or later our structures built of unsuitable material had collapsed yet again.

Wir waren froh, als unser Zug endlich weiter fuhr.

We were glad when our train finally moved along.

Aber schon nach wenigen Stunden hielten wir wieder.

But after only a few hours, we stopped again.

Es war mitten in der Nacht.

It was the middle of the night.

Wir froren entsetzlich und durften uns doch keine Bewegung machen, solange der Zug stand; zu leicht konnte die Aufmerksamkeit des Zugpersonals auf uns gelenkt werden.

We froze horribly and still could not make any motion as long as the train stood still; the attention of the train personnel could have been roused too easily.

Gegen Morgen ging es ein kurzes Stück weiter, dann standen wir wieder.

Toward morning it went a little bit farther, then we stopped again.

Der Zug wurde aufgelöst und unser Waggon auf ein Abstellgleis geschoben; es war der fünfte Tag unserer Fahrt.

The train was uncoupled and our car pushed onto a siding; it was the fifth day of our journey.

Raus konnten wir nicht, denn die Bretterladung hatte sich bereits ganz über den Ausstieg geschoben.

We couldn't get out, because the load of boards had already slid completely over the exit hole.

Wir blickten durch unser Guckloch.

We looked through our peephole.

Draußen lag Schnee, wir sahen einige Gebäude, im Hintergrund Wald.

Outside lay snow, we saw some buildings, in the background a forest.

In der Nähe waren Arbeiter mit dem Beladen anderer Waggons beschäftigt.

Wir blickten uns an, im fahlen Licht konnten wir gerade unsere Gesichtszüge erkennen.

Jeder las die bange Frage des anderen: „Wie lange?"

Close by, there were workers busy loading other cars.

We looked at each other, in the sparse light we could discern the other's facial features.

Each read the anxious question in the other: "How long?"

Durst

„Lange halte ich es nicht mehr aus!

Wenn nicht bald etwas passiert, fange ich an zu schreien, um Hilfe zu rufen.

– Wie lange stehen wir eigentlich schon auf diesem verfl... Abstellgleis?"

„Heute früh waren es drei Tage", entgegnete ich matt.

Drei lange Tage und Nächte – 72 Stunden.

Drei Tage in Ungewißheit und Kälte, drei Tage fast ohne Schlaf, ohne Wasser, ohne etwas zu essen, drei Tage in Dunkelheit oder Zwielicht.

Und noch immer kein Ende abzusehen; ... wer weiß, wann es der Bahnverwaltung einfiel, unseren Waggon weiterzuschicken – er enthielt ja nur „tote Fracht".

Thirst

"I can't hold out much longer!

If something doesn't happen very soon, I'm going to start yelling to call for help.

– How long have we actually been sitting on this blasted siding?"

"As of this morning, it's been three days," I replied dimly.

Three long days and nights – 72 hours.

Three days in uncertainty and cold, three days with almost no sleep, without water, without something to eat, three days in darkness or twilight.

And with no end in sight; ... who knows when it would occur to the train administration to send our car along – it contained only "dead freight."

Am schlimmsten war der Durst; vor zwei Tagen hatten wir den letzten Schluck Kaffee miteinander geteilt, und nun lechzten wir nach etwas Trinkbarem.

Draußen lag Schnee, nur wenige Meter entfernt und doch unerreichbar für uns.

Abwechselnd preßten wir ein Auge an das Guckloch – glaubten die vereinzelnd herniedertanzenden Flocken zu riechen, zu spüren, zu schmecken – und erhöhten doch nur unsere Qual.

Gewiß, wir hätten Lärm schlagen können – man hätte uns herausgeholt und uns zu trinken gegeben, soviel wir gewollt hätten – aber es wäre das Ende unserer Flucht, das Ende der Freiheit gewesen.

Noch war unsere moralische Widerstandskraft stärker als der Durst, noch zwangen wir uns zur Ruhe – aber wie lange noch?

Und freiwillig hatten wir uns in diese Lage begeben; niemand hatte uns dazu veranlaßt, wir selbst hatten es so gewollt.

Warum?

Warum flieht ein Kriegsgefangener überhaupt, wenn er keine physische Not leidet und auch alles getan wird, um die psychische zu lindern?

The worst part was the thirst; two days ago we had divided the last sip of coffee between us, and now we were longing for something drinkable.

Outside lay snow, only a few meters away and yet unreachable for us.

We took turns pressing an eye against the peephole – we thought we could smell, feel and taste the individual flakes coming down – and our distress just climbed.

Sure, we could have made some noise – they would have gotten us out and given us something to drink – but it would have been the end of our escape, the end of our freedom.

Our moral stamina was still stronger than the thirst, we still forced ourselves to keep quiet – but how much longer now?

And we had freely put ourselves into this situation; nobody had forced us into this, we ourselves had so desired it.

Why?

Why does a POW escape anyway, when he suffers no physical emergency and everything is done to ease psychological stress?

Warum vertauscht er ein Leben mit ausreichender Verpflegung in gut geheizten Räumen mit den Gefahren und Entbehrungen einer fast aussichtslosen Flucht?

Why does he trade a life with adequate food in well heated shelter for the danger and hardship of an almost impossible escape?

Brennende Vaterlandsliebe und ein patriotisches Herz waren wohl selten die Triebfeder dazu; gewiß, sie sollen als Beweggründe nicht geleugnet werden;

Burning love of country and a patriotic heart were probably seldom the cause; sure, they shouldn't be denied as reasons;

viel stärkere Motive aber waren wohl in den meisten Fällen Erlebnishunger, Abenteuerlust, Ehrgeiz

but the much stronger motive was indeed in most cases hunger for experience, desire for adventure, ambition

– und der Wunsch, in einem eintönigen Dasein, in dem man selten Leistungen, dafür aber um so mehr menschliche Schwächen zu sehen bekommt,

– and the desire, in a monotonous existence, in which one seldom witnessed achievements, and much more often witnessed human weaknesses,

einmal etwas Besonderes zu zeigen, sich vor den Kameraden zu bewähren.

to once show something special, and prove oneself in front of comrades.

Und schließlich natürlich war es die Sehnsucht nach Freiheit, die wohl nur der richtig verstehen kann, der selbst jahrelang gefangen gewesen ist.

And finally of course it was the longing for freedom, which can probably only be truly understood by those who have themselves been imprisoned for years.

Aber all diese Überlegungen halfen uns nicht weiter.

But all these thoughts didn't help us continue.

Stunde um Stunde verrann, ohne daß Anzeichen für eine Weiterfahrt bemerkbar wurden.

Hour after hour passed, without any noticeable indication for a continued journey.

Unsere Nervosität steigerte sich immer mehr und wegen eines geringfügigen Anlasses begannen wir plötzlich, uns gegenseitig Vorwürfe zu machen.

Our nervousness climbed ever higher and because of some petty thing, we suddenly began to make accusations against each other.

Wir gerieten richtig ins Streiten, was natürlich nur im Flüsterton geschah.

Gerade, als wir in der heftigsten Auseinandersetzung waren, hielten wir plötzlich inne – ein Geräusch hatte unsere Aufmerksamkeit erregt; wir lauschten.

Da, jetzt hörten wir es wieder, irgendwo im Waggon tropfte es!

Sofort war aller Hader verraucht und vergessen, wir wußten später gar nicht mehr, worum sich unser Streit gedreht hatte, wir konzentrierten uns nur noch auf das liebliche Geräusch langsam fallender Wassertropfen.

Bald hatten wir die Stelle gefunden.

Das Dach war dort ein wenig durchrostet und in langsamen Abständen fiel ein Tropfen Schneewasser nach dem anderen hernieder.

Schnell wurde eine leere Konservendose daruntergehalten und das köstliche Naß aufgefangen.

Bald entdeckten wir noch weitere Stellen, durch die es langsam tropfte, und stellten alle nur irgendwie geeignet erscheinenden Gefäße darunter.

We had really started to fight, which of course happened only in whispers.

Then, as the argument was at its most fierce, we suddenly paused – a sound had caught our attention; we listened.

There, now we heard it again, somewhere in the car it was dripping!

Immediately all bickering had subsided and was forgotten, later we didn't even remember what our argument revolved around, we concentrated only on the lovely sound of slowly falling drops of water.

Soon we had found the place.

The roof was a little rusted through there and in slow intervals one drop of melted snow fell down after the other.

Quickly an empty can was held beneath and the precious liquid caught.

Soon we discovered more places that were slowly dripping, and we put all sorts of makeshift containers under them.

Nach einer Stunde konnten wir uns den ersten Schluck frischen Schneewassers genehmigen – er hat uns besser geschmeckt, als der erlesenste Champagner.

Wir waren wie neu geboren; frischer Mut beseelte uns und, um das Glück voll zu machen, legte sich eine Lokomotive vor unseren Waggon und rangierte uns an einen Zug, der sich alsbald in Bewegung setzte.

„Nun aber schnell ein neues Ausstiegloch gesägt", drängte Heinz, „damit wir wenigstens raus können, wenn wir nochmal auf ein totes Gleis geschoben werden."

Viele Möglichkeiten der Auswahl hatten wir allerdings nicht; neben dem blockierten ersten Ausstieg war nur eine kleine Fläche vom Boden freigeblieben.

Dort setzten wir die Säge an und schafften abwechselnd ununterbrochen mehrere Stunden hindurch.

Während der eine sägte, achtete der andere darauf, daß das Schmelzwasser während der Fahrt auch richtig in die Büchsen tropfte.

After an hour, we could each get the first sip of fresh snow water – it tasted better than the choicest champagne.

We were newly reborn; animated with fresh courage, and to complete our luck, a locomotive drove up in front of our car and shunted us to a train, which was quickly set into motion.

"Now quickly cut a new exit hole," urged Heinz, "so we can at least get out if we're again pushed onto a siding."

However, we didn't have many possibilities to choose from; beside the blocked first exit was only a small area of floor left free.

There we set the saw, and taking turns, we worked uninterrupted for several hours to get through.

While one sawed, the other made sure that during the journey the melting snow water dripped directly into the cans.

Eine überraschende Kontrolle

Gegen Abend hielten wir.

Heinz war gerade oben auf den Brettern, während ich, gegen die schwere Schiebtür gelehnt, ein wenig verschnaufte.

Plötzlich hörten wir Stimmen.

Menschen näherten sich unserem Waggon.

Wir vernahmen Hammerschläge gegen den Wagen vor uns – sollten wir schon wieder abgehängt werden …?

Angestrengt lauschten wir …

Da, jetzt kamen sie zu uns, machten sich an der einen Tür unseres Waggons zu schaffen.

Mein Herzschlag stockte, ich hielt den Atem an – suchte man uns?

Hatte man etwas bemerkt?

Wie erstarrt stand ich gegen die Tür gelehnt, während jetzt der Riegel der gegenüberliegenden gelöst und der Waggon geöffnet wurde.

An unexpected inspection

Toward evening, we stopped.

Heinz was directly on top of the boards, while I was leaning against the heavy sliding door, paused for breath.

Suddenly we heard voices.

People approached our car.

We heard the blows of a hammer against the car in front of ours – were we already being uncoupled again …?

We listened intensely …

There, now they came to us, started working to open a door on our freight car.

My heart skipped a beat, I held my breath – were they looking for us?

Had they noticed something?

As if paralyzed, I stood leaning against the door, during which the crossbar on the opposite door was removed and the car was being opened.

Nur die Breite des Wagens trennte mich von den Männern, dazwischen lagen die Bretter.

Dann blitzte eine Taschenlampe auf, ein Mann schwang sich auf den untersten Bretterstapel, leuchtete oberflächlich im Waggon herum.

„Only wood!" – „Nur Holz!" vernahmen wir eine Stimme neben uns.

„Okay" – die Tür wurde zugeschoben, der Riegel vorgelegt und der Waggon wieder plombiert.

Die Männer entfernten sich, untersuchten den nächsten Wagen, den übernächsten …

Schließlich wurde es still.

Allmählich löste sich die Spannung, aber es dauerte eine Weile, bis wir überhaupt ein Wort herausbrachten.

Hätten die Zollbeamten die andere Türe geöffnet, an der ich gestanden hatte … noch jetzt lief es mir heiß und kalt über den Rücken, wenn ich daran dachte.

Ja, es waren Zollbeamte gewesen, die den Zug untersucht hatten.

Wir waren an der Grenze nach USA.

Nach einigen Stunden ging es in südlicher Richtung weiter; unentdeckt hatten wir die Grenze passiert.

Only the width of the car separated me from the men, in between lay the boards.

Then a flashlight lit up, a man climbed onto the lowest stack of boards, shined the light perfunctorily around the car.

"Only wood!" we heard a voice next to us.

"Okay" – the door was pushed shut, the crossbar put back and the car resealed.

The men departed, examined the next car, the one after that …

Finally it was quiet.

Gradually the tension eased, but it took a while until we even uttered a single word.

Had the customs officers opened the other door, where I was leaning … even now I get hot and cold chills up my back when I think about it.

Yes, it was customs officers that had inspected the train.

We were at the border of the USA.

After a few hours it continued in a southerly direction; we had passed through the border undetected.

Nun gab es nicht mehr viele Aufenthalte.

Am nächsten Tag erreichten wir bereits Duluth am Oberen See.

Der Hafen war schon eisfrei, und wir konnten aus unserer winzigen Perspektive einen kleinen Eindruck von der gewaltigen Größe dieses bedeutenden Umschlagplatzes mitnehmen.

Wieder wurde unser Zug aufgelöst und neu zusammengestellt.

Das Rangieren dabei wirkte sich höchst verhängnisvoll für uns aus, denn die Brettermassen schoben sich dabei auch über das zweite mühsam fertiggestellte Ausstiegloch.

Now there weren't many more stops.

The next day we had already reached Duluth on Lake Superior.

The port was already free of ice, and from our tiny window we were able to get a small impression of the awesome size of this prominent trans-shipment center.

Again our train was disbanded and reassembled.

The maneuvering here was quite disastrous for us, because the mass of boards also slid over the second laboriously completed exit hole.

XI

Unsere Lage wird kritisch

Unsere Lage wurde kritisch.

Ein neues Loch konnten wir nicht mehr sägen, denn der Boden war nirgends mehr frei.

Tausende von Brettern hatten sich darübergeschoben.

Einen Versuch, die Bretter von der einen Seite auf die andere umzupacken, mußten wir bald als völlig hoffnungslos aufgeben – wir hätten Wochen dazu benötigt; zudem hatten wir seit drei Tagen so gut wie nichts mehr gegessen.

Verzweifelt sahen wir uns nach anderen Möglichkeiten um, uns aus unserem Gefängnis zu befreien.

Our situation becomes critical

Our situation became critical.

We couldn't saw a new hole anymore, because nowhere on the floor was exposed.

Thousands of boards had slid over.

An attempt to re-stack the boards from one side to the other was quickly given up as completely hopeless – we would have needed weeks; besides for three days we had next to nothing to eat.

Desperately we tried to think up other possibilities for freeing ourselves from our prison.

Durch das Dach konnten wir mit unserem primitiven Werkzeug nicht gelangen, desgleichen nicht durch die Seitenwände, denn die dicken Eichenbohlen waren anscheinend außen noch mit Bandeisen beschlagen.

We couldn't exit through the roof with our primitive tools, likewise not through the side walls, because the thick oak boards were apparently reinforced from the outside with strip steel.

Auf der Suche nach einem Ausgang krochen wir bis ans Ende des Waggons und konnten dort feststellen, daß sich die Fracht um etwa 1 Meter von der Stirnwand des Wagens abgesetzt hatte.

In the search for an exit we crawled up toward the end of the car and could see that the freight had moved about 1 meter away from the front wall of the car.

Hoffnungsvoll ließen wir uns in den Hohlraum hinunter, entzündeten unser Lichtstümpfchen und fanden unten nur zwei Lagen Bretter, die sich nicht verschoben hatten.

Full of hope, we crawled down into the space, lit our candle and found that only two layers of boards hadn't shifted.

„Die letzte Chance zum Rauskommen", sagte ich und machte mich unverzüglich an die Arbeit.

"The last chance to get out," I said and applied myself directly to the work.

Bald waren die beiden Bretter gelöst, und wir hatten den eigentlichen Boden erreicht.

Soon the two boards were removed, and we had reached the actual floor.

Jetzt schnell das Stemmeisen, um ein Loch zu schlagen, damit man die Säge ansetzen konnte.

Now, quickly, the crowbar, to break a hole in the floor so we can use the saw.

„Ja, Heinz, wo ist denn das Stemmeisen?"

"Hey, Heinz, where's that crowbar?"

„Mußt du haben – ich hab doch das Licht mitgenommen und den Hammer."

"You must have it – I carried the light and the hammer."

Verzweifeltes Suchen überall am Boden …

A desperate search all over the floor …

92

„Ich kann es nicht finden; es wird oben liegen geblieben sein; schnell, wir wollen es holen."

"I can't find it; it must have been left up top; quick, we have to get it."

Als wir uns aufrichteten, um nach oben zu klettern, stießen wir mit dem Kopf gegen Bretter.

As we rose to climb up top, our heads crashed against boards.

„Nanu, was ist denn das …?

"Hey, what is that …?

Es ist doch noch gar nicht lange her, da sind wir hier runtergestiegen?!"

It hasn't been all that long since we climbed down here?!"

Im flackernden Kerzenschein sehen wir uns an; Schweißtropfen treten uns auf die Stirn, Röte wechselt mit Blässe.

We looked at each other in the glowing candlelight; sweat beaded on our foreheads, redness swapped with paleness.

Unterdessen braust der Zug durch die Nacht.

Meanwhile the train charged through the night.

Gleichmäßig singen die Räder ihre Melodie, immer die gleiche Strophe: Zu – En – de, zu – En – de, zu – En – de …

Monotonously the wheels sung their melody, always the same verse: It's – o – ver, it's – o – ver, it's – o – ver …

Wirklich zu Ende …?

Was it really over …?

Nein, wir wollen leben, wir wollen raus.

No, we want to live, we want out.

Mit der Kraft der Verzweiflung stemmten wir uns gegen die Bretter über uns – Umsonst! Vergeblich!

Powered by despair we threw ourselves against the boards above us – For nothing! In vain!

Leicht vibrieren die Holzmassen; kaum merklich, aber stetig schieben sie sich auf uns zu, die oberen schneller, so daß sie schon die Wand erreicht haben, die unteren langsamer, infolge ihrer schweren Belastung.

The layers of wood vibrated lightly; hardly noticeable, but steadily they slid toward us, the top ones faster, so that they had already reached the wall, the bottom ones slower, due to the heavy load.

Wie von weit her hören wir das tiefe Heulen der Lokomotive, Weichengeratter folgt, anscheinend ein Bahnhof, das Läutewerk einer Bahnschranke dringt an unser Ohr.

As from afar, we heard the deep howling of the locomotive, the switch plate rattle followed, apparently a train station, the signal bell of a railway crossing gate rang in our ears.

Weiter geht es mit unverminderter Geschwindigkeit, singen die Räder die gleiche Melodie, dieselbe Strophe.

The journey continued with undiminished speed, the wheels sang the same melody, the same verse.

Rasend schnell kreisten die Gedanken.

Our thoughts circled frantically.

Irgendetwas mußten wir tun, nur nicht untätig gegenüber den langsam auf uns zurückenden Holzmassen bleiben.

We must do something, we couldn't just stand idle against the mass of wood slowly moving toward us.

Nun ging auch noch das Licht aus; der Kerzenstumpf war zu Ende …

Now the light went out; the candle stump was at the end …

Einige Streichhölzer besaßen wir noch.

We still had some matches.

Wir schnitten Späne von einem der Bretter, entzündeten sie einen am andern, suchten den Boden, die Wand ab.

We cut shavings from one of the boards, lit them up together, scanned the floor and wall.

„Da, dort der Nagel, den müssen wir rauskriegen."

"There, that nail, we have to get that out."

Es war ein krummgeschlagener Nagel in einer Bohle; mühsam lockerten wir ihn etwas, drehten ihn hin und her und konnten ihn schließlich herausziehen.

It was a bent nail in a board; with great effort we loosened it somewhat, turned it back and forth and could finally pull it out.

Er mußte das Stemmeisen ersetzen.

It had to substitute for the crowbar.

Während einer leuchtete, löste der andere mit diesem provisorischen Werkzeug Span um Span aus einem der dicken Bodenbretter, schaffte mit unendlicher Mühe und blutigen Fingern schließlich ein Loch in den Boden.

While one provided light, the other dug with this make-shift tool, shaving after shaving out of one of the thick floorboards, managing with ceaseless effort and bloody fingers to finally make a hole in the floor.

Endlich waren wir durch das Holz – aber, was war das?

At last we were through the wood – but, what was that?

– es ging nicht tiefer, der Nagel stieß auf Widerstand, auf – Eisen!

– it went no deeper, the nail had hit resistance, from – iron!

Wir hätten weinen können vor grenzenloser Enttäuschung; oder taten wir es?

We could have cried from boundless frustration; or did we?

Ich weiß es nicht mehr.

I don't know any more.

Ich weiß nur, daß uns die Verzweiflung alle Kräfte aufbieten ließ, an einer anderen Stelle zu versuchen, durch den Boden zu gelangen.

I only know that our desperation let us muster all our strength to try to get through the floor in a different spot.

Zweimal noch war es vergeblich, beide Male stieß der Nagel auf Stahlunterzüge, die wahrscheinlich zur Befestigung der Kupplung dienten – wir waren ja an der Stirnseite des Waggons.

Twice more it was futile, both times the nail hit a steel beam, which probably served to secure the coupling – we were after all at the front of the car.

Und pausenlos ging die Fahrt durch die Nacht; Stunde um Stunde – bald fehlte uns jeder Zeitbegriff – wir sahen nur die heranrückenden Holzmassen – 80 cm, 70 cm, 60 cm Raum blieb uns noch – konnten wir es überhaupt noch schaffen, ehe sie uns erdrückten?

Without pause, the ride continued through the night; hour after hour – soon we had lost all track of time – we only saw the nearing masses of wood – only 80 centimeters, 70 centimeters, 60 centimeters of space were left – could we still make it, before they crushed us?

Endlich gelang es uns, eine Stelle zu finden, an der wir nicht auf Eisen unter dem Holz stießen.

Finally we succeeded in finding a spot where we didn't strike iron beneath the wood.

Sogleich setzten wir die Säge an, arbeiteten fieberhaft mit dem Tod um die Wette.

Immediately we applied the saw, working feverishly in a race with death.

Wir mußten es schaffen, es war die einzige Möglichkeit einer Rettung.

We had to make it, it was the only possibility of salvation.

Rufen und Schreien wäre im Fahrtenlärm verhallt; niemand hätte uns gehört.

Yells and screams would been lost against the train noise; no one would have heard us.

Langsam rückten die Holzmassen näher

Slowly the mass of wood moved nearer

Langsam wurde die Öffnung größer – langsam rückten aber auch die Holzmassen näher.

Slowly the opening became bigger – but slowly the mass of wood moved nearer too.

Würde es gelingen?

Would it work?

… und würde der Zug auch noch halten, bevor es zu spät war …?

… and would the train even stop before it was too late …?

Es mochte schon tief in der Nacht sein, und wir waren fast fertig, als wir auf einem Bahnhof einliefen und hielten.

It was well into the night, and we were almost done, when we entered a train station and stopped.

Wir atmeten auf; die Station konnte unsere Rettung sein, denn wenn wir uns unserer Kleider entledigten, mußte es gelingen, sich durch die fast fertige Öffnung hindurchzuzwängen.

We sighed in relief; the station could be our salvation, because if we removed our clothes we should be able to squeeze through the nearly completed opening.

Aber noch ehe wir dazu kamen, ging wieder ein anhaltendes Rangieren los; hin und her wurden wir geschoben, wobei man nicht gerade behutsam mit uns umging.

Beim ersten Ruck bekamen wir etwas Luft und unsere Hoffnung wuchs, der nächste engte unseren Raum wieder ein, und so ging es dauernd hin und her;

mit panischem Schrecken registrierten wir jede Bewegung, die die Holzmassen auf uns zu machten und mit einem Seufzer der Erleichterung diejenigen, die uns wieder Raum gaben.

Einmal wurde ein anderer Waggon mit solcher Wucht gegen uns geschoben, daß sich durch den Anprall die etwa 30 Tonnen Schnittholz in Bewegung setzten und der gesamte soeben gewonnene Raum auf einmal verloren ging.

Wenige Zentimeter vor unseren Köpfen kamen die Bretter zum Stehen.

Das Blut stockte uns in den Adern, für Sekunden setzte der Herzschlag aus – dann hatten wir uns wieder gefangen.

Ohne Rücksicht darauf, ob ein Bahnbeamter vorbeikam oder nicht, versuchten wir ins Freie zu gelangen.

Nur raus hier, ob man uns dabei erwischte oder nicht, war uns jetzt einerlei.

But before we got to it, another series of rerouting maneuvers began; back and forth we were shoved, they weren't being gentle with us.

With the first push, we gained some room and our hopes grew, the next squeezed our space back again, and that's how it continued, back and forth;

we reacted with panicked fright to every movement the mass of wood made toward us, and gave a sigh of relief for those that gave us space again.

Once, another car was pushed against us with such force, that the impact set the roughly 30 tons of boards in motion and the entire space we gained was lost all at once.

A few centimeters from our heads, the boards came to rest.

Our blood curdled, for seconds our hearts stopped beating – we were trapped again.

Without even checking whether or not a railway official was going by, we tried to get out.

Just out of here; whether someone then caught us or not, was now all the same to us.

Bis zu den Hüften zwängte ich mich in die Öffnung – dann saß ich fest; es ging beim besten Willen nicht.

Unter Zurücklassung einiger Hautfetzen mußte ich mich wieder zurückziehen.

Dann versuchte es Heinz; er war schmächtiger und kam weiter.

Aber obgleich er alles ausgezogen hatte, schaffte auch er es nicht; sein Brustkorb war zu breit.

„Ich kann nicht mehr vor und zurück", stöhnte er gequält; er saß fest eingeklemmt zwischen den Bohlen.

Ich packte ihn an den Armen und zog ihn unter Aufbietung aller Kräfte zurück.

Es war höchste Zeit gewesen, denn schon wurden wir weiterrangiert, diesmal glücklicherweise in der anderen Richtung, so daß sich das Holz beim Anrucken wieder etwas von uns absetzte.

Dann schien der Zug fertig zusammengestellt zu sein.

Es wurde still.

Von einer in der Nähe stehenden Lampe des Bahnkörpers drang schwacher Lichtschein durch die Öffnung im Boden in unser Verlies.

In Hockstellung saßen wir uns gegenüber, auf der einen Seite die Stirnwand des Waggons, auf der anderen die drohende Bretterwand.

I forced myself into the opening up to my hips – then I was stuck; no amount of will could get me farther.

At the cost of some layers of skin, I was forced to retreat.

Then Heinz tried; he was lankier and went farther.

But even though he had stripped, he couldn't make it either; his chest was too broad.

"I can no longer move back and forth," he moaned in distress; he was firmly jammed between the boards.

I grasped him by the arms and pulled him back with all my strength.

It was just in time, because we were already being rearranged further, this time luckily in the other direction, so the wood moved a little away from us again when we got jolted.

Then the train seems to have been completely put together.

It became quiet.

From one of the railway lamps standing nearby, a weak light penetrated through the opening in the floor into our dungeon.

In a crouch, we sat facing each other, on one side the front wall of the car, on the other the menacing wall of boards.

Wir sahen unsere blassen Gesichter und lasen die Verzweiflung in unseren Zügen.

Keiner sprach ein Wort.

Plötzlich vernahmen wir Schritte, die sich langsam unserem Waggon näherten; wir sahen den Lichtkegel einer Taschenlampe mehrmals über die Schienen unter uns huschen.

Hatte man uns bemerkt?

Das Herz schlug uns bis zum Hals.

Sollten wir jetzt noch entdeckt werden; jetzt, wo wir in einer Viertelstunde das Loch genügend vergrößern konnten, um bequem zu entschlüpfen?

Oder war es nicht vernünftiger, sich erkennen zu geben und dadurch zwar die Flucht aufzugeben, aber der Lebensgefahr zu entgehen.

Wir schielten zur drohenden Bretterwand, die beim letzten Rangierstoß etwas zurückgewichen war, uns wieder ein wenig Luft lassend – wir blickten uns an – keiner schrie, keiner rief um Hilfe.

Langsam verloren sich die Schritte in der Ferne.

Wir riskierten viel, wir riskierten alles in jener Nacht.

Wir vertrauten auf unser Glück und setzten alles auf eine Karte.

We saw each other's pale faces and read the despair in our features.

Neither spoke a word.

Suddenly we heard steps, that slowly approached our car; we saw the conical beam of a flashlight repeatedly scanning the tracks below us.

Had they noticed us?

Our hearts pounded in our throats.

Should we be caught now; now, where we could have widened the hole enough in fifteen minutes to comfortably slip out?

Or was it not more sensible to reveal ourselves and thus give up our flight, but also escape our life-threatening situation.

We peered at the menacing wall of wood that had slipped backwards with the impact of the car's last transfer, giving us a little room again – we looked at each other – neither yelled, neither called for help.

Slowly the steps were lost in the distance.

We risked a lot, we risked everything that night.

We relied on our luck and put it all on the line.

Wir wollten uns die Chance, unerkannt mehr als 2000 Kilometer von jener Gegend entfernt, in der man uns suchte, unterzutauchen, nicht entgehen lassen.

We didn't want to pass up the chance to hide more than 2000 kilometers away from the area where they were looking for us.

Es war Leichtsinn, sträflicher Leichtsinn sogar;

It was foolishness, wanton foolishness really;

wir spielten mit unserem Leben, denn wenn es uns auch gelingen sollte, in kurzer Frist nach der Abfahrt das Loch genügend zu vergrößern, so hätten wir im Notfall doch nicht während der Fahrt hinausgekonnt,

we gambled with our lives, because even if we should succeed, within a short period after departure, in making the hole big enough, in an emergency we still could not have gotten out while moving,

wir hätten bis zum nächsten Aufenthalt warten müssen – und ob uns die Holzmassen bis dahin am Leben ließen …?

we would have had to wait for the next stop – and whether the mass of wood would let us live until then …?

Langsam vergingen die Stunden; durch die Öffnung zog eisige Kälte.

Slowly the hours went by; a freezing cold streamed in through the opening.

Und doch durften wir uns nicht bewegen, durften nicht sägen, um kein Geräusch zu verursachen.

And still we could not move, could not saw, in order to make no noise.

Wir froren entsetzlich.

We froze horribly.

Allmählich wurden unsere Beine bis zum Unterleib kalt und gefühllos; Blutstockungen traten ein.

Gradually our legs became cold and numb up to our belly; stagnation of the blood set in.

Endlich begann es zu dämmern.

Finally the day began to dawn.

Was würde werden?

What would happen?

Ob wir wohl weiterfuhren oder noch einen Tag stehen blieben?

Would we indeed move on or remain standing for another day?

Gegen acht konnten wir aus gewissen Geräuschen an den Bremsen schließen, daß sich der Zug auf die Abfahrt vorbereitete.

Wir waren aufs höchste gespannt, in welcher Richtung wir fahren würden, denn davon hing alles ab.

Da, jetzt hörten wir den heulenden Pfeifton der Lokomotive, der so viel tiefer ist, als der unserer europäischen Maschinen.

Gleich würde es losgehen, angespannt lauschten wir.

Jetzt vernahmen wir das sich rasch fortsetzende Geräusch der vorn angezogenen Wagenkette,

– jetzt hatte es uns erreicht, setzte sich weiter nach rückwärts fort – wir fuhren, wir fuhren in umgekehrter Richtung, als wir eingelaufen waren,

– wir hatten gewagt und, wenn nicht noch besonders unglückliche Umstände eintreten – gewonnen.

Vor Freude wären wir uns beinahe um den Hals gefallen, aber das war schon aus Raumgründen nicht möglich.

Es war schon schwierig genug, mit unseren steifen Gliedern auf dem engen Raum die Vergrößerung des Loches vorzunehmen.

Aber wir fuhren wieder, konnten jetzt weitersägen, und durch diese Bewegung kam unser Blutkreislauf wieder einigermaßen in Ordnung.

About eight, we could tell from certain noises coming from the brakes that the train was preparing for departure.

We had the utmost anxiety, in which direction would we go, because everything depended on it.

There, now we heard the howling whistle of the locomotive, which is so much deeper than that of our European machines.

Soon it would get going, we listened intensely.

Now we heard the quickly spreading sound of the chain of cars being pulled from the front,

– now it reached us, continued along toward the rear – we moved, we moved in the reverse direction,

– we had taken a risk and, if no particular unfortunate circumstance interfered – had won.

We almost hugged each other out of joy, but it was not possible due to the lack of space.

It was already hard enough with our stiff limbs to work at widening the hole in such a tight space.

But we were moving again, could now saw again, and through this activity our blood flow was again fairly normal.

Bald waren wir mit der Arbeit fertig.

Soon we were finished with the work.

„Ich hänge mal den Kopf nach unten hinaus, vielleicht kann ich etwas von der Gegend erkennen", schlug ich vor.

"I'll stick my head out underneath, maybe I can discern something of our surroundings," I suggested.

Heinz hielt mich an Beinen und Unterleib fest, und ich schaute mich um.

Heinz held fast to my legs and abdomen, and I looked around.

„Links von uns ist ein Meer", berichtete ich, „wir fahren direkt an der Küste entlang."

"The ocean is on our left," I reported, "we're riding right on the coast."

„Am Atlantik können wir aber unmöglich schon sein; seit Duluth sind wir doch erst einen Tag unterwegs", entgegnete Heinz.

"We can't possibly be on the Atlantic Ocean already; we're only a day's distance away from Duluth," replied Heinz.

Wir studierten unsere Karte und fanden bald heraus, daß wir an der Westküste des Michigan-Sees entlang fuhren.

We studied our map and soon figured out, that we were riding along the western coast of Lake Michigan.

Wir hatten ein mörderisches Tempo drauf, so daß unser Waggon nur so schwankte.

We were at breakneck speed, so our car swayed back and forth.

Aber dadurch rutschte die Holzladung immer weiter von uns fort und schließlich konnten wir sogar wieder aufrecht stehen.

But with that, the wood slid farther away from us and finally we could even stand straight up again.

Wir fuhren den ganzen Tag über mit unveränderter Geschwindigkeit.

We traveled the entire day with unwavering speed.

Gegen Abend kamen wir in belebtere Gegenden; unsere Geschwindigkeit wurde verlangsamt, wir hörten Fabriksirenen, Autohupe, Klingeln von Eisenbahnschranken; immer häufiger vernahmen wir das Brüllen von Vieh aus anderen Zügen.

Toward evening we reached more populated areas; our speed was reduced, we heard factory sirens, car horns, the ring of railroad crossings; ever more frequently we heard bellows of cattle from other trains.

„Ich glaube, wir sind bereits in den Außenbezirken von Chicago", folgerte Heinz, „das Vieh ist sicherlich für die Schlachthäuser bestimmt."

"I think we're already on the outskirts of Chicago," concluded Heinz, "the cattle are certainly destined for the slaughterhouses."

„Besser können wir es zum Aussteigen gar nicht treffen", erwiderte ich, „hier in der Großstadt tauchen wir am besten unter."

"We couldn't have hit a better spot to get off," I replied, "here in the big city is the best place to disappear."

Es war schon dunkel, als wir endlich hielten.

It was already dark when we finally arrived.

Aufmerksam lauschten wir; immer wieder kamen Bahnbeamte vorbei, klopften an den Rädern, sahen die Bremsen nach.

Alert, we listened; train personnel kept passing by, banging the wheels, checking the brakes.

Endlich schien die Kontrolle beendet.

Finally the inspection seemed to be over.

XII

Wir verlassen den Waggon

„Jetzt wird es Zeit, sonst fahren wir wieder los", flüsterte ich und schob mich durch die Öffnung; Heinz folgte.

Rasch versuchten wir nach rechts zu entweichen.

Da kam uns plötzlich ein Bahnbeamter entgegen.

Schnell verschwanden wir wieder unter dem Zug und versuchten es auf der anderen Seite.

Dort schien die Luft rein.

Wir torkelten mehr als wir gingen zwischen zwei Zügen entlang; ganz steif waren unsere Glieder vom langen Hocken.

Vor zehn Tagen waren wir in den Waggon gestiegen – endlich waren wir wieder heraus.

We leave the freight car

"Now it's time, otherwise we'll be moving again," I whispered, and slid through the opening; Heinz followed.

Moving quickly, we tried to escape to the right.

There was suddenly a railway official heading our way.

Swiftly we disappeared back under the train and tried it on the other side.

There the coast seemed clear.

We staggered more than walked, going between two trains; our joints were quite stiff from crouching so long.

Ten days ago we'd gotten in the car – finally we were out again.

In einiger Entfernung vor uns sahen wir Lichter über die Gleise huschen.

Some distance ahead of us we saw lights hovering over the tracks.

„Dort muß ein Bahnübergang sein", raunte ich Heinz zu und trieb zur Eile, „wenn wir den unangefochten erreichen, dann sind wir sicher."

"That must be a railroad crossing," I murmured to Heinz and pressed on, "if we reach it unseen, then we're safe."

Plötzlich sehen wir uns einem Bahnarbeiter gegenüber, wir konnten nicht mehr ausweichen, er hatte uns bereits erblickt.

Suddenly we saw a railway worker across from us; we couldn't escape, he had already spotted us.

Also draufzu.

Let's just go.

Dicht gingen wir an ihm vorbei, husteten, schnäuzten die Nase – er nahm gar nicht Notiz von uns, glaubte wahrscheinlich, daß wir hierher gehörten.

Close by, we went past him, coughed, blew our noses – he took absolutely no notice of us, probably thought that we belonged here.

Nur jetzt nicht hasten, ruhig weitergehen, damit wir nicht auffallen.

Don't rush now, calmly continue, so we don't attract attention.

So, das wäre noch mal gut gegangen.

So, that was something else that went well.

Bald hatten wir den Bahnübergang erreicht, schalteten uns in den Fußgängerstrom ein und tauchten im Großstadtgewimmel unter.

Soon we reached the railway crossing, fell in line with the stream of pedestrians and disappeared into the swarm of the big city.

„Mein Gott!" flüsterte Heinz, „diese glücklichen Menschen!"

"My God!" whispered Heinz, "these happy people!"

Wir schritten durch hellerleuchtete Straßen; von den Dächern und aus den Schaufenstern warb eine verschwenderische Lichtreklame; gut angezogene Menschen in Feiertagsstimmung begegneten uns; luxuriöse Kraftwagen fuhren an uns vorüber

We strode through brightly lit streets; extravagant neon signs advertised from rooftops and display windows; we encountered well dressed people full of cheerful holiday spirit; luxurious cars drove past us

– es war ein Bild, wie wir es seit Jahren nicht mehr gesehen hatten.

Wir freuten uns an allem, was wir sahen und eine Glücksstimmung überkam uns, die sich kaum beschreiben läßt.

In der Sicherheit der großen Stadt bummelten wir gemächlich durch die belebten Straßen.

Erst als wir die herrlichen Auslagen eines Lebensmittelgeschäftes betrachteten, machte sich der Hunger wieder bemerkbar – der Magen verlangte entschieden sein Recht, und wir gingen auf die Suche nach einem Hotel.

Aber es waren nur gute, elegante und teure Häuser, die man uns empfahl.

Wir waren schon müde, als wir endlich in einer Seitenstraße ein kleines Hotel fanden, dessen Portier uns ein Doppelbett für zwei Dollar anbot.

Wir atmeten auf, als er keine Vorauszahlung verlangte, denn wir besaßen ja nur kanadisches Geld, und um diese Stunde waren die Banken längst zu.

Ob wir wohl auch ein Abendessen bekommen könnten, fragten wir beiläufig und hatten Mühe, dabei ruhig zu bleiben.

Nein, sie führten keine Küche, kam die Antwort.

– it was a picture we hadn't seen in many years.

We found joy in everything that we saw and a happy mood overcame us, one that can hardly be described.

In the safety of the big city we meandered leisurely through the busy streets.

Only when we saw the delicious displays of goods in the grocery stores did our hunger become noticeable – our stomachs demanded their due, and we went on the search for a hotel.

But only nice, elegant and expensive guesthouses were recommended to us.

We were already tired when we finally found a small hotel on a side street, whose porter offered us a double bed for two dollars.

We breathed a sigh of relief when he didn't require a down payment, since we only had Canadian money and at this hour the banks were long closed.

We casually asked whether we could also get some dinner, and in the process had to make an effort to stay calm.

No, they didn't have a kitchen, came the answer.

Die Enttäuschung war grenzenlos; rasch gingen wir auf unser Zimmer, um unseren furchtbaren Hunger nicht merken zu lassen.

Our disappointment knew no bounds; we quickly walked to our room, so that our terrible hunger would not be noticed.

Unter der heißen Dusche reinigten wir uns vom Schmutz der letzten Tage, gingen zu Bett und fielen bald in tiefen, traumlosen Schlaf.

Under a hot shower we cleaned ourselves of the dirt from the last few days, went to bed and soon fell into a deep, dreamless sleep.

Im Omnibus nach Gary (Indiana)

On the bus to Gary (Indiana)

Es war herzlich wenig, was wir am nächsten Tage für unser kanadisches Geld gewechselt erhielten.

We received precious little when we exchanged our Canadian money the next day.

Es langte gerade für die Hotelrechnung, ein Frühstück in der nächsten Speisebar und zur Omnibusfahrt nach Gary, wo wir in der großen Carnegie Steel Corporation Arbeit zu finden hofften, denn wir hatten eine entsprechende Annonce gelesen.

It was barely enough for the hotel bill, breakfast in the neighboring diner and the bus ride to Gary, where we hoped to find work in the big Carnegie Steel Corporation, something we had read in a help wanted ad.

Wir hatten den Omnibus kaum verlassen und schlenderten unschlüssig durch die nächsten Straßen, noch nicht recht wissend, wohin wir uns wenden sollten – da kreischten Bremsen, ein Wagen hielt neben uns, dem ein Herr im leichten Sommermantel entstieg und auf uns zukam.

We had barely gotten off the bus and were walking the streets a little uncertain, not yet really knowing where we should go – when brakes screeched, a car stopped next to us, then a gentleman wearing a light summer coat got out and walked up to us.

Was der nur von uns wollte?

What could he want from us?

Einen Augenblick wich das Blut aus unseren Gesichtern, dann hatten wir uns gefaßt.

„Well boys", begann er sogleich die Unterhaltung, „Ihr seht gerade so aus, als ob ihr Arbeit suchtet; ich hätte einen guten Job für euch."

Erstaunt blickten wir uns an; suchte man so in Amerika Arbeiter?

Waren die Arbeitskräfte so rar?

Was er uns denn zu bieten habe, fragten wir.

Er heiße Kretlow und sei der Manager eines Walzwerkes von Carnegie.

„Wir suchen dringend Arbeiter, auch für die Nachkriegszeit bereits.

1 Dollar 20 die Stunde kann ich euch bieten, wenn ihr ungelernt seid; in einem Vierteljahr bekommt ihr 1,70; Überstunden werden doppelt bezahlt."

Das ließ sich hören.

„Wir seien nicht abgeneigt, aber wir kämen aus Kanada."

„Oh, das macht nichts, wir beschäftigen viele Ausländer.

Geht nur aufs Arbeitsamt und sagt, daß wir euch einstellen.

Hier habt ihr meine Telefonnummer."

For a moment, the blood disappeared from our faces, but we quickly composed ourselves.

"Well boys," he began the conversation at once, "You look like you're searching for work; I have a good job for you."

Astonished, we looked at each other; that is how they look for workers in America?

Was the workforce that scarce?

We asked him what he had to offer us.

His name was Kretlow and he was the manager of a Carnegie steel mill.

"We're desperately seeking workers, also for the postwar period.

1 Dollar 20 an hour I can offer you, if you're unskilled; in a quarter of a year you'll be making $1.70; overtime will be paid double."

That sounded good.

"We're not averse, but we are from Canada."

"Oh, that doesn't matter; we employ many foreigners.

Just go to the unemployment office and say that we'll hire you.

Here, have my telephone number."

Er drückte uns seine Karte in die Hand und mit den Worten: „See you later", verschwand er so schnell, wie er gekommen war.

Das amerikanische Arbeitsamt, das wir in Gary kennenlernten, hat einen guten Eindruck bei mir hinterlassen.

Wir wurden sehr höflich und zuvorkommend behandelt, es gab keine Schranke, über die hinüber man seine Personalien angeben mußte, es wurden uns Stühle am Tisch unseres Sachbearbeiters angeboten ...

und in keinem Augenblick während der Unterhaltung hatten wir das Gefühl, als Bittsteller behandelt zu werden.

Es waren auch zahlreiche Schwarze im Raum, ich konnte aber keinen Unterschied in ihrer Abfertigung feststellen.

Nachdem man unsere Ausweise geprüft und für gut befunden hatte, gab man sich alle Mühe, uns so schnell wie möglich die erforderlichen Papiere zur Arbeitsaufnahme auszustellen.

Hierfür waren nur noch einige Rückfragen bei Mr. Kretlow, dem Manager des Walzwerkes nötig.

Immer wieder versuchte unser Sachbearbeiter, ihn telefonisch zu erreichen, leider vergeblich.

He pressed his business card in our hands and with the words: "See you later," he left as quickly as he had come.

The American unemployment office that we visited in Gary left a good impression on me.

We were treated with politeness and courtesy; nothing forced us to give any personal information, we were offered chairs at our clerk's desk ...

and at no point during the conversation did we have the feeling of being treated like we were soliciting something.

There were a lot of black people in the room too, but I couldn't tell any difference in how they were being treated.

After they had checked our IDs and found them to be valid, great efforts were made to get us the necessary documents to be able to start work as quickly as possible.

In order to accomplish this, a few calls were made to Mr. Kretlow, manager of the steel mill.

Again and again our clerk tried to reach him by telephone, to no avail.

Schließlich bat er uns, am Montag wiederzukommen (es war Freitag), wir würden dann unsere Papiere erhalten und gleich mit der Arbeit beginnen können.

Wir dankten ihm für seine Bemühungen und verließen das Amt.

Es war später Nachmittag; gemächlich schlenderten wir durch die Straßen; mit Genuß betrachteten wir die schönen Auslagen in den Schaufenstern; dabei hatten die Lebensmittelgeschäfte eine besondere Anziehungskraft.

„Herr Gott, hab' ich einen Hunger!" murmelte Heinz, „und keinen Cent mehr in der Tasche.

Wo kriegen wir bloß etwas Geld her?"

„Meine Uhr muß dran glauben", sagte ich kurz entschlossen und schon hatte ich die Klinke eines Uhrengeschäftes in der Hand.

„Bullova Watches" stand in geschwungener Schrift über den blitzenden Glasscheiben, hinter denen viele kostbare Uhren lagen und ein Mr. Deutsch war der Inhaber des Geschäftes.

„Ausgerechnet Deutsch heißt der Mann", flüsterte ich, „hoffentlich bringt uns das Glück."

Finally he asked us to come back on Monday (it was Friday), we would receive our papers and could start work immediately.

We thanked him for his efforts and left the office.

It was late afternoon; slowly we roamed through the streets; we enjoyed the nice displays in the shop windows; here the grocery stores had a special appeal.

"Dear God, I'm so hungry!" muttered Heinz, "and not a cent left in my pocket.

Now where can we get some money?"

"My watch must make the sacrifice," I said determined and already had the door handle of a watch shop in my hand.

"Bullova Watches" read a rolling sign above the sparkling glass windows, behind which were many expensive watches and the owner of the shop, a Mr. Deutsch.

"Of all things, the man's name is Deutsch," I whispered, "hopefully it will bring us luck."

111

Es war eine gute Uhr, die wir anboten, ein Schweizer, kein deutsches Fabrikat, das Verdacht hätte erregen können.

Lange hielt sie der Ladeninhaber in der Hand und sein Auge betrachtete nicht nur das tickende Räderwerk, sondern glitt auch an unseren Gestalten auf und nieder.

Endlich gab er uns die Uhr zurück: „Wir verkaufen Uhren, aber wir kaufen grundsätzlich keine.

Vielleicht versuchen sie es einmal bei meiner Konkurrenz um die Ecke; ich glaube, dort haben sie Aussicht."

Es wiederholte sich dieselbe Szene,

der Mann hielt die Uhr in der Hand, und über die Lupe hinweg musterte er uns aufmerksam,

während er – scheinbar zufällig – mit seinem Angestellten, der sich an der Tür postiert hatte, über zwei Juwelendiebe sprach, die Chicagos Geschäftsstraßen unsicher machten.

It was a good watch that we had to offer, a Swiss model, not German made, which might have aroused suspicion.

The owner held it in his hand for a long time and his eye not only looked over the ticking clockwork, but also up and down our figures.

Finally he handed us the watch back: "We sell watches, but we buy basically none.

Maybe you can try our competition around the corner; I think you might be successful there."

The same scene was repeated,

the man held the watch in his hand and he examined us while peering over his magnifying glass,

during which – a supposed coincidence – he talked to his employee, who had positioned himself in the doorway, about two jewelry robbers who made Chicago's business district unsafe.

XIII

Wieder gefangen

Plötzlich riß der Angestellte die Tür auf.

Zwei Kriminalbeamte erschienen und verlangten unsere Papiere.

Dies aber, das wußten wir, ist in Amerika so ungewöhnlich, daß es schon fast einer Überführung gleichkommt.

Captured again

Suddenly the employee yanked the door open.

Two detectives entered and asked for our papers.

This was, we knew, so unusual in America that it almost always meant an arrest was coming.

Daß wir mit den Juwelendieben nichts zu tun hatten, ergab sofort ein Vergleich mit den Steckbriefen der Gesuchten auf der Wache.

That we had nothing to do with the jewelry heists was immediately determined with a comparison to the wanted posters at the police station.

Da fragte der Beamte geradezu: „Weshalb sind sie nicht in der Armee?"

Then one of the detectives asked: "For what reason are you not in the army?"

Nein, Freundchen, so fängst du uns nicht!

No, pal, you're not going to catch us that way!

Jeder von uns hatte sich eine genaue „story", einen Lebenslauf zurechtgelegt, an den wir schon fast selbst glaubten,

Each of us had concocted a precise "story," a résumé, which we almost believed ourselves by now,

– so oft hatten wir ihn uns hergesagt, und es brachte uns auch nicht in Verlegenheit, als im Kreuzverhör Querfragen auf uns einprasselten, die unsere Kenntnis der Orte und Personen, von denen wir sprachen, auf die Probe stellten.

– we had practiced it so often that it didn't present any difficulty even under cross-examination when they tested our knowledge about the locations and people we talked about.

Schon halb beruhigt, bat der Beamte höflich um unsere Brieftaschen.

Somewhat calmer, the detective asked us politely for our wallets.

„Nanu, sie besitzen ja überhaupt keinen Cent?"

"Hey, you don't have even a single cent?"

Sein Mißtrauen war aufs neue geweckt, „Ziehen sie sich mal aus!" befahl er.

His suspicion was aroused anew, "Get undressed!" he commanded.

„Sonderbar, diese ungefütterte Jacke", bemerkte er zu seinem Kollegen, „sieh dir mal die Overalls der Burschen an, wer weiß, wo sie die her haben."

"Odd, this unlined jacket," he remarked to his colleague, "look at the overalls of these guys; who knows where they got them from."

Fast war schon alles gut vorüber, da stutzte er plötzlich: „Wie kommt dieser knallrote Stoff in die Naht?"

Interessiert schaute der andere Beamte hinüber: „Oh, jetzt weiß ich's, sie sind Kriegsgefangene aus Kanada, dort ist ihre Kleidung zur besonderen Kenntlichmachung mit roten Flecken und Streifen versehen."

„Gute Miene zum bösen Spiel machen!" sage ich zu Heinz

– und zum Polizisten: „You won – sie haben gewonnen!

Gratuliere zu ihrem Scharfsinn."

Der nahm die dargebotene Hand an, aber nachdem unsere richtigen Personalien notiert und unsere Fingerabdrücke genommen waren, steckte man uns in Gefängniszellen.

Peinlich wurde es erst in den Verhören, die am nächsten Tage begannen.

Uhrendiebe waren wir nicht, Deserteure auch nicht; aber daß wir als deutsche Kriegsgefangene über 2000 km ausgerechnet ins Herz der amerikanischen Rüstungsindustrie geflohen waren, erschien merkwürdig, höchst merkwürdig, geradezu verdächtig.

Wir mußten Saboteure sein!

Everything was almost over, when he paused suddenly: "How did this red fabric get into the seam?"

Interested, the other detective looked over: "Oh, now I know; they're POWs from Canada, there the clothing is marked with red spots and stripes for easy recognition."

"Let's make the best of a bad situation!" I say to Heinz

– and to the policeman: "You won! Congratulations for being so sharp."

He shook my outstretched hand, but after our real personal information was written down and our fingerprints were taken, they put us into jail cells.

It only became embarrassing during the interrogation that began the next day.

We were not watch thieves, also not deserters; but that we as German POWs had fled over 2000 kilometers right into the heart of the American defense industry, seemed strange, quite strange, outright suspicious.

We must be saboteurs!

„Der Flucht seid ihr schon überführt!"
sagte der alte Hase der „FBI", des
Federal Bureau of Investigation.

"You're already guilty of escaping!"
said the old detective from the FBI.

„Gesteht, was ihr sonst noch
verbrochen und vorgehabt habt!"

"Confess, what else you've done
and what you were planning!"

Es wurde ein langes Verhör, dem sich
noch viele weitere anschlossen, bis
man sich schließlich im Verlaufe einer
Woche davon überzeugt hatte, daß
wir wirklich nur harmlose
Kriegsgefangene waren, denen
Sabotage oder Spionageabsichten
gänzlich fern gelegen hatten.

It became a long interrogation, then
followed by many more, until finally
over the course of a week we had
convinced them, that we were truly
only harmless prisoners of war, who
had no interest in sabotage or
espionage.

**Ausgebrochene deutsche
Kriegsgefangene aufgegriffen**

„Der Polizist Eduard Urban nimmt
Fingerabdrücke von Lt. Heinz Meuche
und Lt. Klaus Conrad, deutschen
Offizieren, die nach ihrer Flucht am 3.
März aus einem kanadischen
Kriegsgefangenenlager in Gary
aufgegriffen wurden."

(Aus Chicago Tribune
  von 21. 4. 1945)

**Escaped German
POWs apprehended**

"Police officer Eduard Urban takes
the fingerprints of Lt. Heinz Meuche
and Lt. Klaus Conrad, German
officers, who were apprehended in
Gary after their March 3rd escape
from a Canadian POW camp."

(From the Chicago Tribune
  of April 21, 1945)

Zurück nach Kanada

Und dann kam der Tag, an dem man uns wieder nach Kanada brachte.

Es war eine schöne Fahrt von Chicago nach Detroit;

wir saßen recht komfortabel in dem 1.-Klasse-Abteil, sehr viel bequemer, als in unserem Güterwagen voller Bretter, und der uns begleitende Leutnant und die beiden Sergeanten waren höflich und korrekt

– aber sie erinnerten uns eben doch immer daran, daß wir nun wieder Gefangene waren und so dachten wir manchmal doch wehmütig an unseren Güterzug zurück, in dem wir zwar eingeengt, aber frei waren.

In Detroit übergab man uns den kanadischen Behörden.

Spät in der Nacht erreichten wir unseren Bestimmungsort, das Lager Gravenhurst nördlich von Toronto im Staate Ontario.

Am nächsten Tag wurden wir dem Kommandanten vorgeführt.

„Well, sie haben einen schönen Trip gemacht, meine Hochachtung!" sagte er zur Begrüßung, „aber um vier Wochen Arrest kommen sie nicht herum; regulations, I can't help it – da kann man nichts machen."

Back to Canada

And then came the day we were taken back to Canada.

It was a nice ride from Chicago to Detroit;

we sat quite comfortably in the first class compartment, very much nicer than our freight car full of boards, and the lieutenant and both sergeants accompanying us were polite and proper

– but still they reminded us always that we were now prisoners again and so we sometimes thought wistfully back to our freight train, in which we were cramped, but were free.

In Detroit we were handed over to the Canadian authorities.

Late at night we reached our destination, Camp Gravenhurst, north of Toronto in the province of Ontario.

The next day we were brought before the commander.

"Well, you've taken a nice trip; my highest regards!" he said as greeting, "but you can't get around four weeks of confinement; regulations, I can't help it."

„Wir sind uns darüber im klaren", entgegnete Heinz.

"We realize that," replied Heinz.

„Gut", sagte er – und sich an seinen Adjutanten wendend, „sorgen sie dafür, daß man den beiden etwas zu Lesen gibt."

"Good," he said – and turning to his adjutant, "take care that both are given something to read."

Als wir schon an der Tür waren, rief er uns noch einmal zurück.

When we were at the door, he called us back once more.

„Nach den Bestimmungen ist Kriegsgefangenen im Arrest das Rauchen verboten; sie rauchen doch?" wendete er sich an mich.

"According to the regulations, POWs aren't allowed to smoke while in confinement; you smoke, right?" he turned to me.

„Ja, Sir, allerdings nur Zigarren!"

"Yes sir, however just cigars!"

„I'm sorry – es tut mir leid; ich glaube kaum, daß ich da etwas für sie tun kann."

"I'm sorry; but I don't think I can do anything for you there."

Aber vom nächsten Tage an schickte er mir täglich zwei Zigarren in die Zelle.

But from the next day onward he sent two cigars daily to my cell.

Appendix

**Original-Kampfbericht aus dem Archiv
des britischen Verteidigungsministeriums
vom 10. April 1941**

**Original war report from the archive
of the British Ministry of Defence
from April 10, 1941**

Combat Report.

10.4.41   "B" Flight, 264 Squadron.   F/O Barwell.

Enemy aircraft: He 111   Time of attack: 2135 hrs.

Place of attack: Uncertain point approximately over coast at Beachy Head.

Range and duration of firing: Three or four bursts of 1 to 2 seconds from 300 yards to 50 yards underneath.

General Report:

I took off with Sgt. Martin as gunner from Biggin Hill at 2015 hrs on 10.4.41 to patrol the Kenley Sector. This I did at heights varying between 14-18,000 ft. I was vectored after an e/a and whilst at about 15,000 ft saw the Bandit 500 ft above me and about 1,000 yards ahead flying on the same course.

I closed to 300 yards on the beam and slightly underneath and Sgt. Martin opened fire. He got in about four good bursts of one or two seconds each whilst we were closing in from 300 to 50 yards and we both saw the de Wilde ammunition bursting in the fuselage and engines.

E/a took evasive action by putting his nose up and climbing so that even at 120 m.p.h. when the Defiant was almost stalling, we were still overshooting.

As we passed underneath the enemy aircraft it could clearly be distinguished as a He 111 and Sgt. Martin had ceased fire as he had been blinded by the flashes of his ammunition. At this moment the e/a suddenly dived almost vertically into the cloud below and although I followed him I never saw him again. As I came out through the cloud which was about 500 ft thick at 10,000 ft I saw the incendiaries from the e/a strike the ground between Redhill and Beachy Head. I now understand that the e/a crashed near the coast and that the crew baled out, which neither I or my gunner had observed. There was no return fire throughout the combat. We claim one He 111 destroyed. We fired 435 rounds of ammunition and landed back at Tangmere at 2215 hrs. Controlled by G.L. Kenley, which was excellent.

(Signed)   Barwell.

F/O. "B" Flight, 264 Squadron.

Note: This crew took off on a second sortie from Tangmere at 0238 hrs on 11.4.41 and at 0330 engaged another He 111 at 7,000 ft over Beachy Head. This e/a was claimed probably destroyed. Defiant landed back at Biggin Hill.

und wie ich es erlebte ...

Wir waren am 10. April 1941 gegen 19 Uhr in Paris mit Ziel Liverpool gestartet, um dort Hafenanlagen zu bombadieren.

Um 21 Uhr 15 überflogen wir die englische Südküste in 5000 m und befanden uns um 21 Uhr 35 westlich von London in 6000 m Höhe.

Plötzlich gab es einen Knall und eine Erschütterung; ich glaubte, eine Flakgranate habe uns getroffen, doch wenige Sekunden später sah ich gegen den Nachthimmel die Silhouette eines Nachtjägers.

Der Knall rührte von einem Feuerstoß aus seiner 2 cm-Vierlingskanone her (Typ Defiant).

In der Maschine war einiges zerstört, Splitter hatten den Bordschützen Eckert verletzt; über mir war eine Ölleitung getroffen und das Öl lief über meine Beine in die Pelzstiefel.

Aber unsere He 111 war noch manövrierfähig, die meisten Instrumente intakt und die Bordsprechanlage funktionierte.

Der Nachtjäger setzte aus einer Steilkurve zu einem zweiten Angriff an; ich stellte die Maschinen auf den Kopf und entkam ihm etwa 1000 m tiefer in einer Wolkenbank.

and how I experienced it ...

On April 10th, 1941 around 7 p.m., we had taken off from Paris with destination Liverpool, to bomb seaport facilities there.

Around 9:15 p.m. we flew over the English south coast at 5000 meters and around 9:35 p.m. found ourselves west of London at 6000 meters altitude.

Suddenly there was a bang and a shock; I thought an anti-aircraft grenade had hit us, but only a few seconds later I saw the outline of a night fighter against the night sky.

The bang came from a burst of fire from his 2-centimeter, 4-gun turret (type Defiant).

Several things in the aircraft were damaged, splinters had wounded the gunner, Eckert; above me an oil pipe had been hit and the oil ran down my legs into my fleece boots.

But our He 111 was still maneuverable, most of the instrument panel intact and the intercom worked.

The night fighter set out on a steep curve to make a second attack; I turned the aircraft on its head and escaped him about 1000 meters lower, in a bank of clouds.

Dort fing ich die He 111 so sanft ab, wie ich nur konnte, um ein Abmontieren der Flächen nach dem Sturzflug zu vermeiden.

There I pulled the He 111 up as gently as I possibly could, to prevent severe damage to the wings after the nosedive.

Ich ging dann auf Gegenkurs, ließ die Bomben im Notwurf abwerfen und einen Funkspruch absetzen, daß wir versuchen würden, den Kanal zu erreichen, wo uns der Seenotdienst auffischen sollte.

I flew a reciprocal course, performed an emergency bomb drop and transmitted a radio message that we would try to reach the channel, where sea rescue should fish us out.

Doch schon bald ging die Tourenzahl des linken Motors zurück, der Ölkühler war zerschossen, der Motor fraß und fing an zu brennen.

But soon the rpm count of the left engine went down, the oil cooler was shot, the engine stopped and caught on fire.

Mit dem rechten Motor hielt ich die Maschine noch zehn Minuten, dann brannte er auch.

With the right engine, I held the aircraft up another ten minutes, then it caught fire too.

Nun ging es in ziemlich steilem Gleitflug abwärts; bei 800 m Höhe gab ich Befehl zum Aussteigen; Bordschütze Eckert und Funker Schwarzer sprangen zuerst, unser Kriegsberichter Karl-August Richter brauchte etwas länger.

Now it was going down at quite a steep gliding angle; at 800 meters altitude I gave the command to abandon the aircraft; gunner Eckert and radio operator Schwarzer jumped first, our war reporter Karl-August Richter needed somewhat longer.

Mein Beobachter, Oberfeldwebel Platt hatte die Nerven verloren und wollte ohne Schirm springen.

My observer, Staff Sergeant Platt had lost his nerve and intended to jump without a parachute.

Ich riß ihn zurück, er klinkte den Brustfallschirm ein und sprang aus der Kanzel.

I yanked him back, he put his parachute on and jumped out of the cockpit.

Ich spürte einen Ruck, er mußte gegen das Leitwerk geschlagen sein, sein Schirm öffnete sich nicht.

I felt a jerk, he must have hit against the tail, his parachute didn't open.

Wertvolle Höhe war verloren gegangen.

Valuable altitude had been lost.

Ich schnallte mich los, wollte hinterher, sah, daß der Höhenmesser nur noch 80 m zeigte, errechnete blitzschnell, daß ich nur noch 40 m über Grund war, weil die englische Südküste 80 m über NN, Paris aber nur 40 m über NN liegt.

Ich setzte mich wieder ans Steuer, fand in der Dunkelheit eine Wiese, die ich mehr ahnte, als sah und machte mit der seit 20 Minuten brennenden Maschine mitten zwischen dort gegen Luftlandeeinheiten aufgestellten Autowracks eine Bauchlandung.

Obgleich nicht mehr angeschnallt konnte ich mich im Sitz halten.

Die Maschine machte einen „Ringelpietz", überschlug sich aber nicht.

Ich sprang unverletzt heraus, warf Karten und Codeunterlagen ins Feuer und lief in Richtung der nahen Küste; gleich darauf explodierte die He 111 hinter mir.

Ich lief weiter, hörte Schüsse, jemand schrie „Hands up", ich war umstellt und geriet in Gefangenschaft.

Es war 22 Uhr am Gründonnerstag 1941.

I unstrapped, wanted to follow, saw that the altimeter showed a mere 80 meters, calculated at lightning speed that I was just 40 meters above ground, because the south coast of England was itself 80 meters above sea level and Paris was just 40 meters above sea level.

I sat down at the controls again, found a field of grass in the darkness, well, I assumed more than saw, and made a belly landing with a machine that had been burning for 20 minutes; I landed between scrap cars put there as measures against airborne units.

Even though I wasn't buckled in I managed to stay in my seat.

The machine spun around but didn't turn over.

I jumped out unharmed, threw maps and code documents into the fire and ran in the direction of the nearby coast; shortly afterwards the He 111 exploded behind me.

I ran farther, heard shots, somebody yelled "Hands up," I was surrounded and taken captive.

It was 10 p.m. on Holy Thursday of 1941.

Afterword

If you enjoyed the book, **please tell your friends!** We published it in order to share what I think is both a compelling story and an interesting bit of history. I also want to make bilingual books more common, and more supportive of the challenge of learning another language.

You might also consider sending a quick note for us to forward to the author. It may encourage him **to write down some additional "escapades"** – including the true story of an encounter in England with the father of a now-famous ... well, any more information might give the game away.

Scott S. Lawton
November 2009

Germancosm
24 Colonial Dr.
Chelmsford, MA 01824

Visit **can-esc.com** for the latest news and links

Made in the USA
Lexington, KY
26 May 2010